**A STUDY GUIDE
COMMENTARY**

LEVITICUS

D1603236

A STUDY GUIDE COMMENTARY

LEVITICUS

LOUIS GOLDBERG

ZONDERVAN
PUBLISHING HOUSE OF THE ZONDERVAN CORPORATION
GRAND RAPIDS, MICHIGAN 49506

LEVITICUS: A STUDY GUIDE COMMENTARY
© 1980 by The Zondervan Corporation
Grand Rapids, Michigan

Library of Congress Cataloging in Publication Data

Goldberg, Louis, 1923-
    Leviticus, a study guide commentary.

        1. Bible.   O. T.   Leviticus—Commentaries.
2. Bible.   O. T.   Leviticus—study.   I.   Title.
BS1225.3.G59   222'.1307   80-16837
ISBN 0-310-41813-5

Scripture references in this book are from the *Holy Bible: New International Version.*
Copyright © 1978 by the New York Bible Society. Used by permission of Zondervan
Bible Publishers.

All rights reserved. No part of this publication may be reproduced, stored in a retrieval
system, or transmitted in any form or by any means electronic, mechanical, photocopy,
recording or otherwise, without the prior permission of the publisher.

Printed in the United States of America

22.1307
564L

L.I.F.E. College Library
1100 Glendale Blvd.
Los Angeles. Calif. 90026

Contents

027587

L.I.F.E. College Library
Los Angeles, Calif. 90026

Preface

This commentary on Leviticus comes out of a detailed study of the book through the years. My love for the Torah and for Jewish traditions began when I was a boy in an Orthodox Jewish home and has continued through my seminary training, after I acknowledged Jesus as my Messiah and Redeemer. It was my privilege in the congregations I served as pastor to teach and to preach from Leviticus many times. In so doing, I inculcated in believers a love for that portion of the Word, an understanding of the basic background of the life and work of Jesus the Messiah, and an appreciation of the personal application of the book today. I intensified my study of Leviticus while I was teaching the book as part of a course in the Pentateuch to students at Moody Bible Institute. I was gratified to see that the spirituality of the students developed while they were engaged in a close examination of Leviticus.

In writing this book, I have prayed that many readers will gain a deeper knowledge of the way the Law undergirds the ministry of Jesus the Messiah and the way it can lead to a closer walk with the Lord.

Acknowledgments

I pay grateful tribute to the teachers who had a part in my Jewish heritage, as well as to Dr. Arnold Schultz, under whom I was privileged to study the Hebrew Scriptures (Old Testament) while in the Northern Baptist Theological Seminary. I wish to express my sincerest appreciation to Norma Hadrava, a faithful and dear friend in one of the congregations I served, for her stenographic work on the first draft, and to Callie Kniceley for typing the final copy. I want to acknowledge the appreciation of affectionate and eager students of the Pentateuch, from whom I have learned much. Last, but not least, I am thankful to God for the prayers of a loving wife, who is my help in the ministry.

Introduction

The Book of Leviticus is a closed book for most Christians. The commands for slaughter of animals, the descriptions of priestly ritual, the classifications of what one was to wear and eat, and the lack of narrative all make for uninteresting reading—so some people think. The tragic practice of many Christians is to avoid Leviticus, but they miss the great blessings that accompany an understanding of the basics and background of our faith. It is my sincere hope that this commentary on Leviticus will open a storehouse of joy and blessing for many people.

Leviticus deals with the Mosaic covenant, or constitution, which consisted of three major parts: the moral, the sacrificial, and the juridical (legal). A fourth area defined specific models of worship and dimensions of life style, e.g., the Sabbath, dietary, cleanliness, etc. All four parts served as the rule and guide for every aspect of life, but it was the first three which uniquely established the Mosaic constitution. The moral aspect provided the ethical absolutes for maintaining a godly life style. The sacrificial system set forth the great lessons of salvation from sin, dedication to God, and thanksgiving to and fellowship with Him. The juridical part was the system whereby the nation handled its civil and criminal claims. Certain passages in Exodus spell out the three elements included in the constitution, and in Leviticus each of these is expanded. With the coming of Messiah, and with His dying as an atonement for sin, the sacrificial element of the constitution was fulfilled. The Mosaic covenant was eventually to merge into the New Covenant of the messianic kingdom.

Significantly, Leviticus stands in the middle of the Books of Moses to provide information as to how Israel should worship Yahweh. The family of Jacob had become a nation while in bondage in Egypt, and as a free people they needed instruction on how to worship Yahweh, who was not merely a tribal or a national deity but who was the God of the whole earth. This great omnipotent God had revealed Himself as a holy God, so it was necessary that Israel know how to approach Him. Leviticus declares the holiness of God and describes preparations necessary in order to worship Him.

That only a handful of Jewish people recognized that Jesus was Messiah was no fault of the Mosaic constitution; men had added their traditions to the Word so that in some significant areas it had become minimized and obscured (Mark 7:9, 13). The Mosaic covenant was to be the schoolmaster that would lead Israel to her Messiah (Gal. 3:24). Consequently, the Book of Leviticus abounds in types that are definitely linked to His person, ministry, and death. A *type* is a historical person, object, or event that has, in addition to its historical significance, a divinely intended future significance. It foreshadows a corresponding person, object, or event, known as an *antitype*. Types are useful and important in understanding the relationship of Leviticus to Messiah's ministry.

A further word needs to be said concerning types. Many who approach Leviticus do not pay careful attention to the meaning of the book for the Israelites but instead deal only with the types. Such emphasis on types frequently is excessive. It is important not to invent types that cannot be substantiated by sound exegesis. Types are limited to only two categories, and any supposed type that does not fit one of these two categories is not legitimate. A type can be substantiated when the New Testament designates it as one. An example is that of Adam (the type) and Jesus (the antitype). The New Testament clearly shows a relationship between Adam, the head of the human race, and Christ, the head of the new creation (1 Cor. 15:45).

A second category allows for types that are not explicitly designated as such but are strongly implied. One example of such a type is that of Isaac (the type) and Jesus (the antitype). In Genesis 22:2 we read that Isaac, Abraham's only son, was to be offered up as a sacrifice. The similarity between that verse and John 3:16, in which God's only Son is said to have been offered up, strongly implies a typical relationship.

Obviously, naming as types only persons, objects, and events so designated or implied puts a restriction on our finding of types and also prevents excessive typifying and careless exegesis. Our study in Leviticus will demonstrate that even while following these strict guidelines, we may discover a wealth of types.

Modern culture, unlike that of Old Testament culture, is not built on a sacrificial system. Consequently, many people today question the necessity of sacrifices. Of course, the Christian is aware that Christ's death was a sacrifice, but if he does not understand the Old Testament sacrificial system, he misses much of the significance of Christ's sacrifice.

Prior to the Fall, Adam and Eve had perfect fellowship with God. There were no barriers between the Lord and them. They were completely and totally consecrated to living within God's perfect will, and therefore enjoyed perfect bliss with the Lord as their friend and confidant.

After the Fall (Gen. 3) that perfect fellowship was broken. The act of sin, the eating of the forbidden fruit, put Adam and Eve outside God's will. Sweet communion between Creator and creature was shattered, and the trauma of separation was magnified when God called, "Where are you?" (Gen. 3:9).

How to get back into the circle of God's fellowship has been man's problem from that day to this. It seems evident that God revealed to Adam and Eve the fact that sacrifice was needed for atonement. There is a hint of a sacrifice in Genesis 3:21, although God's stated desire was to clothe Adam and Eve. Some aspect of the Incarnation may also have been revealed. There is a note of expectation in Eve's declaration at the birth of Cain, when she said, "I have gotten a man, the Lord" (Gen. 4:1, lit.). God's principle of a substitutionary sacrifice for sin was perverted with the passing of time, but there continued in succeeding generations man's desperate emptiness and spiritual longing that resulted from the loss of his unbroken fellowship with the Lord. Man, when he had any religion at all, invented his own religious systems to try to fill that emptiness. But these systems were built entirely on works. Man was trying, in essence, to redeem himself with his own good works and without regard to God's system of substitutionary blood sacrifice.

Leviticus was penned to provide precise guidelines for sacrifice, worship, and service primarily for an elect nation but also for Gentiles who would trust in and submit to Israel's God. Leviticus clearly sets forth and institutionalizes the system of substitutionary blood sacrifice. Regardless of how one may argue, God has established the principles of sacrifice. Not to accept His specific revelation concerning sacrifice will do irreparable harm to the soul.

Author

It is not our purpose to refute the critical theories against the Mosaic authorship of Leviticus. Scripture itself testifies that Moses was the God-appointed writer. Leviticus 1:1 says, "The LORD called to Moses and spoke to him." The implication is that what follows is Moses' record of what the Lord said. The Lord Jesus affirmed the Mosaic authorship of Leviticus when in Matthew 8:4 He told the healed lepers to show themselves to the priest and to present the offering Moses had prescribed. The only place in the entire Old Testament where an offering is prescribed for a cured leper is Leviticus 14:10–32. Jesus repeatedly affirmed the Mosaic authorship of the Law (see John 5:46–47), and Leviticus is an integral part of the Law. It seems clear, therefore, that according to Scripture itself Moses was the author of Leviticus.

Recipients

There were two groups of people to whom Leviticus was specifically addressed. One was composed of the sons of Israel (1:2; 4:2; 7:23; and 11:2); the other was Aaron and his descendants, who were to act as priests for the sons of Israel (6:9; 8:2).

Date

The date of Leviticus is established from dates given in other books of the Pentateuch. The first Passover occurred on the fourteenth day of the first month of the Exodus (Nisan, corresponding to our March-April time of year). (See Exod. 12:2, 3, 6.) The tabernacle was erected about one year later, on the first day of the first month in the second year (Exod. 40:17). The Israelites began their journey to Canaan in the next month (Num. 10:11). Therefore Leviticus must have been given to Moses some time toward the end of the first year after leaving Egypt (c. 1446, B.C., if one takes the early date for Exodus).

Purpose, Theme, and Title

The purpose of Leviticus has already been touched on, but there are some more specific points to consider.

First, Israel as an elect people were to be kept separate from pagan nations and were to be "shut up to" God. Leviticus was a code of laws that would not only regulate every detail of the Israelites' lives but would also make Israel different from other nations.

Second, Leviticus revealed to Israel the holiness of God (19:2). All the other characteristics of God, such as His righteousness, truthfulness, faithfulness, mercy and love, are closely related to His holiness, and holiness may be considered the very essence of God. Leviticus stresses His holiness and insists that His people be holy.

Third, Leviticus outlined a system of sacrifices that revealed God's way of salvation. Although many Christians think that Israel knew only law and legalism, the sacrificial system revealed the great mercy and grace of God. Through the sacrifices Israelites could understand how to know the Lord and how to serve Him with singleness of purpose and heart.

Finally, Israel was to be a blessing to all peoples of the earth. There is enough evidence to demonstrate the fact that many strangers and foreigners from pagan nations became Israelites through conversion when they saw the blessing of the true God upon His people Israel. They grasped the meaning of salvation in the Levitical system, accepted it, and therefore became a part of the people of Israel.

The theme of the book tells how an elect, holy people should worship a holy God. The English title, Leviticus, comes from the Septuagint, where the word refers to the Levitical book that provided instructions for Aaron and his sons as to how to function as priests. Hebrew titles for the biblical books come from the first word or the first two words of the book. The Hebrew title for Leviticus is *vayikra* ("and He called").

Key Words

The key words in Leviticus are "holy" (used eighty-seven times), "atonement" (used forty-nine times), and "sacrifice," (counting "offering" and "oblation," used approximately three hundred times). The central lesson of the book is summed up in the phrase: "It is the blood that makes atonement for one's life" (Lev. 17:11).

Outline

Introduction
- A. Authorship
- B. Recipients
- C. Date
- D. Purpose, Theme, and Title
- E. Key Words

Chapter 1: Law of the Offerings With Individual Regulations (1:1–6:7)
- A. The Law of the Burnt Offering (1:1–17)
- B. The Law of the Grain Offering (2:1–16)
- C. The Law of the Fellowship Offering (3:1–17; 7:12–18)
- D. The Law of the Sin Offering (4:1–5:13)
- E. The Law of the Trespass Offering (5:14–6:7)

Chapter 2: Law of the Offerings With Regulations for the Priests (6:8–7:30)
- A. Burnt Offering (6:8–13)
- B. Grain Offering (6:14–18)
- C. Grain Offering When High Priests Were Consecrated (6:19–23)
- D. Sin Offering (6:24–30)
- E. Guilt Offering (7:1–7)
- F. Special Provisions for the Priests (7:8–10)
- G. The Fellowship or Peace Offering (7:11; 7:28–34)
- H. Miscellaneous Instructions (7:19–27)
- I. Conclusion (7:28–38)

Chapter 3: Laws of Priestly Consecration (8:1–10:20)
- A. Consecration of Aaron and His Sons (8:1–36)
- B. Installation of the Priests (9:1–24)
- C. Necessity of Careful Observance of God's Word (10:1–20)

Chapter 4: Laws of Purification (11:1–15:33)
- A. The Diet of God's People (11:1–47)
- B. Laws of Motherhood (12:1–8)
- C. Sanctification and Holiness (13:1–14:57)
- D. Unique Legislation for Body Cleanliness (15:1–33)

Chapter 11: Laws of Vows and Tithes (27:1–34)
    A. Dedication of Persons (27:1–8)
    B. Dedication of Animals (27:9–13)
    C. Dedication of Houses (27:14–15)
    D. Dedication of Fields (27:16–21)
    E. Standard of Value (27:25)
    F. That Which Belongs to the Lord (27:26–34)

For Further Study

1. In a Bible dictionary or encyclopedia (see bibliography) read articles on: holy (holiness), Leviticus, Mosaic covenant (Law of Moses), worship, type.

2. We have seen how man, in order to satisfy an inner emptiness and longing, substitutes a worship system of works righteousness to fulfill his need. Can you name other activities of man to meet his need of inner longing?

3. The holiness of God emphasizes sharply the barrier between the awesome God and sinful man. How did Leviticus explain how God and man can be brought together? Was this limited to Israel only in Old Testament times?

Chapter 1

Law of the Offerings— Individual Regulations

(Leviticus 1:1–6:7)

Before we undertake the exposition and interpretation of the text, we should give a word of explanation about the sequence of the offerings.

Throughout the ancient Middle East during Moses' time, people were aware of and involved with dedicatory and thanksgiving offerings to the deities. The dedication offerings were just one expression of man's attempt to gain the approval of the gods and to be in good-standing with them. The thanksgiving offerings reflected mankind's gratitude to the deities for good fortunes and health. Unregenerate people can and do thank their gods for material blessings.

Chapters 1 and 2 of Leviticus describe God's laws for dedicatory offerings, and chapter 3 sets forth principles for the thanksgiving sacrifice. Chapters 4 through 6:7 describe the sin and trespass offerings. They introduce the idea of a sacrifice for sin, which idea apparently was known to Adam, Eve, and Noah and his three sons, but was written down by Moses, who explains it. Leviticus serves as a constant reminder to succeeding generations of the need for a sacrifice for sin. Human nature being what it is, the tendency to resist or modify the idea of the need for atonement for sin still exists. Man either substitutes his own self-righteous offering for the atonement sacrifice, or he dilutes it with self-righteous efforts.

For that reason chapters 4 and 5 of Leviticus need to be constantly emphasized in every generation to prevent any omission or perversion of the message of salvation and restitution.

To emphasize the place of atonement, the Holy Spirit instructed the Israelites that before they could approach a holy and righteous

God, they had to *begin* with the sin offering of chapter 4 and the offering for trespasses described in chapter 5. These were essential offerings, and only after offering them could the Israelites offer the dedicatory and thanksgiving offerings. In other words, the Israelites were locked into this procedure so that the lesson of salvation would be constantly emphasized.

This royal route of worship was to instruct the Israelites in the way of salvation and service, but the message often fell on deaf ears. Paul eventually said, "Circumcision is circumcision of the heart, by the Spirit" (Rom. 2:29), implying that only a remnant of people who sacrificed really were regenerated. This is not to cast aspersions on Israel; the same thing might be said of Christendom today. Even with the atoning death of Christ as history and with a full revelation of both the Old and the New Testaments in our hands, many churches are filled with unsaved people who are resistant to the grace of God. They substitute their own self-efforts for Christ's sacrifice, and try to earn salvation by works in a procedure contrary to the Word of God.

In connection with the laws governing offerings, we will first examine the procedure of ritual, and then give an interpretation, an explanation, and an application.

A. The Law of the Burnt Offering (1:1–17)

Voluntary offering

God said to Moses, "When any of you brings an offering" (v. 2). The word "when" indicates that this offering is entirely voluntary. The Hebrew word *qorban,* which means "offering" or "gift," stresses the voluntary nature of the burnt offering.

Kinds of sacrifices

When people desired to present a burnt offering, there were three kinds they could offer. According to verse 2 it could be a bull from the herd; according to verse 10 it could be either a male goat or a male sheep; and according to verse 14 it could be a dove or a pigeon. Obviously, there was a decreasing scale of cost from a bull to a pigeon, making it possible for everyone to bring a burnt offering. In His mercy God enabled even the poor man to bring his gift of a pigeon if he desired to offer such a sacrifice. Therefore, the rich were to bring their bulls, the middle class were to offer from their flocks, and the poor could bring their offerings of birds.

But the rich and the middle class were not to present sacrifices of pigeons; to do so would have been an affront to God. Furthermore, since one's actions have consequences that affect others, one person's misdeed might also influence others to follow suit. Offenders were stopped and reprimanded, and their sacrifices were to be rejected by the officiating priest.

Without blemish

All offerings were to be without defects of any kind; they were to conform to God's holy character. Centuries later Malachi still had to chide some people for offering blind, lame, or sick animals (Mal. 1:7, 8). These people would not think of presenting such offerings as gifts to their civil authorities; how could they even think of offering less than the best to their sovereign, holy King? That they did offer animals with defects demonstrated two things: they despised God, and their hearts were evil.

There is still another vital implication involved in the rule that animals to be offered should be without defects. Each of these animals was a type of the One who was to come and fulfill the meaning of the animal sacrifices. Perfection in the animals was a necessary aspect of the type that demonstrated the perfect character and perfect sacrifice of the antitype, Jesus Christ. Imperfect animals could not possibly portray His perfect sacrifice. Only by obeying God's instructions would people ultimately learn of the beautiful tie between the animal, as the type, and Jesus, as the antitype.

Identification

Before the animal was killed, the offerer laid his hands on the head of the sacrifice (v. 4). This ceremony depicted identification. The offerer became identified with the animal, and the animal became a substitute for the offerer. Whatever happened to the animal from this point forward should be seen as having actually been experienced by the Israelite offerer. That is the principle of substitution, an important element in every sacrifice offered to God.

From a biblical point of view, it was not possible to offer human beings as sacrifices because the sin nature was inherent in every person. Until the perfect Man came, offering Himself as the only perfect Sacrifice because there was no sin in Him, animals were used to represent the offerers. The animal is considered amoral, or without a nature to which sin can be charged.

Not a lesson in atonement

In verse 4 mention is made of atonement. We shall not go into the discussion of the meaning of the word atonement until we get to chapters 4 and 16, but suffice it to say here that whereas the main emphasis of the burnt offering of chapter 1 is that of dedication, the main lesson in the sacrifice of chapter 4 is that of atonement. As already indicated, the worship procedure was to start with the atonement for sin described in chapter 4 and the trespass sacrifice (ch. 5); then came the voluntary burnt offering of chapter 1. Therefore, the sacrificial system allowed for no dedication offering until first the atonement for sin was made.

Procedure of the ritual

1. *Slaughtering the offerings.* In every case, except for the offering of birds, the offerer himself killed the animal sacrifice (vv. 5, 11). Perhaps the reason for this was that since the offerer was already identified with the animal, he had to take the action involved in the lesson of the offering. In chapter 1 the lesson of the offering was dedication, and the slaughtering of the animal demonstrated dedication. It was as if the offerer himself laid down his life in dedication before the Lord.

Since the bird was small, the priest handled all the details associated with identification and with the killing and offering of the bird. However, the sacrifice included the same features of identification and substitution as the sacrifice of the bull, goat, or sheep did, despite the slight difference of procedure.

2. *Offering the blood.* The offerer killed the animal, and it was the function of the priest to collect its blood (vv. 5, 11). He presented the blood before the Lord by sprinkling it all around the altar of burnt offering (vv. 5, 11), which stood in front of the tabernacle, and which later in history was in front of the temple.

In the bird offering the small amount of blood was drained on the altar side (v. 15); the blood was *never* to be burnt on the altar. Blood was presented to the Lord in an act that symbolized the death of the animal or the bird even though the sacrifice was never actually killed on the altar. The blood was poured out as a symbol of a life given up. We shall discuss further this relation of blood and life in chapter 17, but it is essential to note that the blood was always sacred to God and was always to be handled in a reverent manner.

3. *Disposal of the carcasses.* The bodies of the bull, the goat, or the sheep were cut in pieces (vv. 8–9, 12–13). The head and the fat (that which burns most easily) were arranged on top of the wood and fire already prepared. The entrails, legs, and feet were washed to remove all the blood. An exception was made with the bull's hide, which belonged to the officiating priest; the expensive hide was something extra for the priest and represented some of God's remuneration for His anointed, officiating servant. Otherwise the animal's carcass was completely consumed on the altar. Only the ashes were removed afterward (see Lev. 6:11).

The officiating priest wrung off the head of the bird offering and placed it on the altar. Removing the head made it easier to drain the blood so that it would not be burned on the altar. The priest then removed the crop and the feathers and flung them into the ashes east of the altar. The crop and feathers were not considered part of the offering. After that the priest tore the bird by the wings without severing the body from the wings, and placed the bird on the altar to be consumed.

Meaning

1. *To the Israelite.* By now you may have sensed the lesson of the burnt offering. We have seen that except for the blood, the bull's hide, the bird's crop, and the feathers the entire animal was consumed on the altar of the burnt offering. The totality of the sacrifice showed the totality of the offerer's consecration as he was identified with the offering. It was a fitting conclusion, after having offered sacrifices for atonement from sin, that the Israelite should voluntarily offer a sacrifice to signify to God that his life was not his own. Then the Israelite was completely given to God for His service.

The design of repetition was to lead the Israelite ultimately to understand the offering's emphasis. There is a danger, however, in simply going through a ritual, and many Israelites did go through the procedure of the offering without permitting its meaning to touch their lives. We face a similar danger in our churches today as we listen to messages over and over again to which we simply do not respond.

2. *In type.* Since the sacrificial system had a messianic significance in typology, the relationship of the dedicatory offering to Jesus Christ cannot be overlooked. Because of our rather strict approach to

the study of types (see the Introduction), we will not examine every supposed similarity or contrast between Old Testament types and New Testament antitypes. The main typological significance of the burnt offering is the relationship of the total dedication of the Old Testament sacrifice to that of Christ's total dedication. In every action the Messiah gave His life in complete consecration to His heavenly Father, for He always did that which pleased His heavenly Father (John 8:29). Ultimately He even drank of the cup of sin in obedience to His Father's will (Matt. 26:39), and voluntarily paid for sin with the price of His own life. His willingness to lay down His life shows the kind of consecration spoken of in the burnt offering.

3. *To believers today.* The lesson of consecration and the typical fulfillment in Christ are both important for us. Paul used the lesson of the burnt offering to remind us that we as believers are to present our bodies as living, holy sacrifices, acceptable to God (Rom. 12:1). We are called upon to lay down our lives in total dedication to Him, knowing that our sins have been forgiven. Such an act of total dedication in the believer's life today relates exactly to the meaning of the Old Testament burnt offering.

B. The Law of the Grain Offering (2:1–16)

The lesson of the burnt offering emphasized only half the concept of dedication. Another lesson was necessary to complete the concept of a genuine consecration for service, and that lesson was taught in the grain offering.

Grain offering (vv. 1–3)

Although in the King James Version of the Bible the offering in chapter 2 is called a meat offering, it has nothing to do with meat. In the days of the King James translators "meat" had a broader meaning than it has today. The Hebrew word *minhah* (or grain offering) of chapter 2 refers to an offering of the produce of the ground. Of all the offerings of Leviticus, it alone entailed no shedding of blood.

1. *Fine flour.* It is best to explain some of the meaning of the grain offering in order to avoid any misunderstanding that might come from the fact that the grain offering was not a blood sacrifice. Think, for a moment, how fine flour is obtained. The farmer breaks up the ground, sows the seed, and then cultivates the ground if it is necessary. He has to wait on God to provide rain at the proper times, and finally he

harvests the crop. He separates the grain from the chaff, and he mills the grain into flour.

When one voluntarily offered his grain offering, therefore, he was presenting a commodity that had been produced through much diligence and hard labor. The portion offered to the Lord represented the total labor needed to produce all of one's grain. Therefore, one aspect of the grain offering was an emphasis on the sanctity of labor. Labor had a relationship to dedication that was blessed by God. It took a bloodless offering to demonstrate that lesson.

In offering this fine flour, the offerer poured oil on it. Oil, of course, moistened the flour so that it would not blow away, especially when it was put on the altar. But the oil also had a symbolic meaning. It was used in the Old Testament for anointing, and it always symbolized the presence of God. The presence of God was upon the offering to bless the consecration of labor on behalf of the Israelite offerer.

Frankincense was also put on the grain offering, and its aroma permeated the air when the offering was burned. The portion of the grain put on the altar gave off a soothing aroma because of the frankincense, symbolizing the fact that God considered the consecrated labor of the offerer worthy to be accepted by Him.

2. *Division of the portion.* The priest took a handful of the flour and placed it on the altar, but the rest of the flour was for the priests' use. All the flour was regarded as offered to the Lord, but God made provision for His servants, the priests, so they could eat from the edibles offered at the altar. We did not see this principle in action in the burnt offering, since the only object an officiating priest could have from that offering was the hide of a bull. But with all other offerings there were portions for the priests. Since the Israelite was never to have the idea that he was directly supporting the priesthood, he brought his offerings *to the Lord.* The Lord, in His grace, then made provision for His servants.

3. *Special preparation of the grain* (vv. 4–10). Many Israelites went a step further with the grain offering and made cakes or wafers from the flour, and ovens, griddles, or pans were used for such preparations. The making of cakes or wafers might be regarded as an added effort of love. The officiating priest offered a memorial portion of the cake or wafer, and the rest was a provision by the Lord for the priests.

Special injunctions (vv. 11–13)

No leaven was to be added to the offering of grain, and of course no leaven was to be used in the preparation of cakes and wafers made from grain. Verse 11 indicates that no grain offering, which would go up in smoke from the altar as an offering to the Lord, could contain leaven (yeast). Since the altar of the burnt offering was one of the meeting places of the Lord and His people (Exod. 29:42), it was a most holy place. Therefore, it was not possible that leaven, which is used as a symbol of impurity, or of evil, in both the Old and the New Testaments, should ever be placed on the altar of His presence. Similarly, no honey was to be added to the grain or prepared with the cakes, since honey was a source of sugar that was used in the fermenting process and was also associated with leaven as a symbol of corruption.

Furthermore, all grain offerings were to contain salt. If any leaven was present unintentionally, the salt would arrest the leavening action and would therefore symbolize the nullification of any presence of sin. Also, the salt, which seasoned the sacrifice, seems to have symbolized God's holiness.

Early ripened things (vv. 14–16)

Israelites were encouraged to bring a grain offering of fresh ripened grain if it was not possible to bring the fine flour. It was an act of grace on God's part to make it possible for anyone voluntarily to offer the grain offering, even if he could not bring prepared cakes or wafers, or even fine flour. The fresh heads of grain were to be roasted, and in offering the roasted grain, oil and incense were placed on the memorial portion to be offered by the priest and burned on the altar as an offering unto the Lord.

Meaning

1. *To the Israelite.* We have already seen the significance of the burnt offering in Israelite worship. But that teaches only half the concept of dedication. It pictures complete dedication of the life to the Lord. *Using* the life given over to the Lord in work for Him is also important, and that truth is vividly pictured in all the labor required in the making of fine flour. Therefore, in the voluntary worship of dedication, once atonement for sin had been made, the burnt offering and the grain offering went together, indicating dedication of both life and labor.

2. *In type.* The grain offering seems to have pictured the Messiah's character and ministry. The fine flour of the grain typified the perfection of the character of Christ. No dimension of Christ's nature—His love, His holiness, His righteousness—was lacking. He was perfect in every way.

All the work involved in obtaining the fine flour for this sacrifice points to the work of Christ. In His ministry He took the difficult path of hard labor and of unselfish service. Christ always did those things that pleased the Father (John 5:36–47). He did His work perfectly, in total dedication to His Father.

God's presence, as symbolized in the oil of the sacrifice, was continually upon Jesus in His life and ministry. His life was well pleasing to God (Matt. 3:17), as is symbolized by the frankincense of the sacrifice. The absence of leaven in the sacrifice pictures His sinlessness. The grain offering, in divine design as a type, pictured perfectly the Son of Man, Jesus the Messiah.

3. *To believers today.* It should not be difficult to see meaning in the grain offering for us today. The farmer of the Old Testament patiently labored to bring forth grain and then offered finely milled flour to the Lord. In like manner we are encouraged to serve the Lord diligently and wholeheartedly. We already saw from the lesson of the burnt offering that we are to lay down our lives in dedication (Rom. 12:1, 2); we are also to *use* these lives in the Lord's service. Our labor for the Lord is sacred, no matter where we are. Every place of employment can be an altar where a dedicated Christian can produce labor that is sanctified and blessed by God.

C. The Law of the Fellowship Offering (3:1–7; 7:12–18)

As already indicated, the peace, or thanksgiving, offering was well-known in the ancient Middle East. Men have always sought to thank their deities for good fortunes. Therefore, they have entertained their deities around banqueting tables. In the Mosaic constitution a fresh outlook and a proper procedure were given for the thanksgiving offering.

Preliminary

Many aspects of the peace offering were the same as those already described under the burnt offering of chapter 1. The peace offering was voluntary (v. 1), as were the dedicatory offerings. The animals were to be without defect (vv. 1 and 6). The identification procedure was the same in both cases; the offerer laid his hands on the heads of the various animals offered (3:2, 8, 13), and the offerer himself killed the animal.

Economic status

Again we see God's grace and mercy in the various choices of animals He allowed for the sacrifice. From the herd either a bull or a cow could be offered (v. 1). From the flock a lamb or a goat, either a male or a female, was permitted to be sacrificed (vv. 6–7, 12). Again, the variations were in accordance with the economic status of the offerer. Animals were required because the peace offering concluded with a ritual meal for the Israelites. A pigeon could not be used because it would not provide a meal for a family or a clan.

Priest's part

As before, it was the priests' function to offer the blood, which is synonymous with life, on the altar of burnt offering. For the peace offering the blood was taken from the animal and sprinkled around the altar of burnt offering (vv. 2, 8, and 13). The blood was regarded as offered before the Lord, but it was never burned.

The animal was then cut in a special way. When treating chapter 7, we shall see how the priests entered into the joyful occasion of the ritual meal by retaining the breast and the right shoulder. The animal was cut in such a way that the fat of the inner parts, the kidneys with their fat, the covering of the liver, and in the case of the sheep, the entire tail down to the backbone, were all removed and offered up in the fire of the altar. The odor was a soothing aroma to the Lord. Herds and flocks that were sleek and fat were generally considered an evidence of the Lord's blessing and a symbol of the Lord's goodness on the land. Physical blessings were also a sign of spiritual blessings, so the fat that was fired on the altar as a pleasing aroma to God served as a reminder that He alone made all blessings possible.

Offering of various cakes

In addition to the giving of animals for the thanksgiving offering, the offerer was to prepare a variety of breads for the feast. But since this was a ritual meal, a portion of the breads was to be offered to the Lord. For the occasion, unleavened cakes mixed with oil, unleavened wafers spread with oil, cakes of well-kneaded flour mixed with oil, and even cakes of leavened bread were brought before the officiating priest (7:12–14). One of each was offered with an up-and-down motion before the altar as a presentation, or heave offering, and that along with the priest's portion of meat (7:34) became the officiating priest's portion in the ritual meal.

Note carefully that none of the breads was actually placed on the altar because leaven was present. One might be puzzled about the use of the leavened bread, but there were at least two reasons for the command to use leaven. First, there was a practical consideration, since leavened bread is more substantial than unleavened. Therefore, allowance was made for this one sacrifice that provided for a ritual feast. Second, there was a spiritual consideration with symbolic meaning since leaven, representing sin, was present to remind the Israelite of his own insufficiencies. Blessings were present because of the living God, who honored His word to provide abundantly for His people.

The ritual meal (7:15–18)

What was left of the peace offering after it was returned to the offerer by the officiating priest was then taken, and at a designated place (usually some home) a feast was prepared. The offerer's immediate family was present, and if the sacrifice was a bull or a cow, the entire family, as well as friends, were invited. All the meat had to be consumed on the day it was offered (v. 15). People gathered to the feast, the blessings of God were remembered, the songs of Zion were sung, and everyone praised God for His goodnesses. People were not only to thank the Lord for material blessings but were also to be grateful for spiritual blessings such as redemption and hope. They were to remember in humility that they, of all the people on the earth, were called as an elect people to be a witness of the word of God to pagan peoples.

Other ritual meals were related to vows and freewill offerings (7:16–18). Vows of all kinds were often sealed with a feast, and it was an opportunity to thank God for the desire to serve or to do something for the Lord in a special way. Freewill offerings were usually given on occasions when many people were present to partake of a feast. These might be festive occasions in families such as weddings, or state occasions such as the dedication of Solomon's temple (1 Kings 8:13–66).

Often vows were made or freewill offerings were given on occasions that lasted a long time. Participants might come from great distances. Therefore, the meals were permitted to last for two days. In any case, no meat of any offering was to be left over for the third day, for by that time meat would begin to turn rancid. It was to be burned, and anyone who dared to eat it committed a grievous sin (vv. 17–18).

Meaning

1. *To the Israelite.* In the order of offerings the peace offering was last. It was a festive occasion—an occasion when the participants remembered and related the blessings of God in their lives. There was a key difference between the festive meals under the Mosaic constitution and pagan, festive meal rites. In the latter the pagans had a sense of "gratitude" to their deities, but the approach to their gods was on a selfish level. In these occasions the people ate and drank in the presence of their deities, and although the people were thankful, they curried the favor of their gods. For the Israelite the festive table was really the Lord's Table. He was the Host, and the Israelites sat at His table while thanking their Benefactor, who had provided for them. The fellowship or thanksgiving offering was intended to be a beautiful and meaningful conclusion to the series of sacrifices performed by the grateful people of Israel.

2. *In type.* The fruit of the ministry of Jesus the Messiah as fulfilled in His death was typified in the peace offering. A possible reference to the peace offering is in Colossians 1:20: "[Christ made] peace through his blood, shed on the cross." Jesus is our peace offering. He made genuine peace possible, for He *is* our peace when we have life through His death (Eph. 2:14).

3. *To believers today.* The taking of Communion today bears a close relationship to the peace offering of the Mosaic constitution. The Lord's Supper affords a formal occasion for believers to remember and to thank God, and in it we are partaking of the elements that represent Christ, who died for us and who made peace for us. We are reminded that He Himslf is the occasion of all our joy and hope.

D. The Law of the Sin Offering (4:1–35; 5:1–13)

Basic to all offerings was the sin offering. Without it there was no way to please God. As we have already indicated, it was the first sacrifice offered in the cycle of offerings. Its teachings about sin, repentance, and salvation were designed to make those concepts uppermost in people's minds and hearts, and its lessons were intended to be preached continually so that people could grasp and appropriate them.

Preliminary

The sin offering and the trespass offering of chapter 5 were required sacrifices. Each offender had to bring his own sacrificial animal if he was guilty of sin. No one was to gloss over sin, and if the offender remained unaware of it, the Day of Atonement offering was to take care of all sin.

Concerning sin

The discussion of the sin offering begins with these words: "When anyone sins unintentionally" (v. 2). That phrase refers to a number of classes of people: the anointed priest who, if he sins brings guilt on the people (v. 3), the congregation that commits error which escapes the notice of the assembly (v. 13), a civil authority who sins unintentionally (v. 22), and anyone among the common people who sins unintentionally (v. 27). Like an ominous note the oft-recurring mention of sin is a constant reminder of man's failure.

Many will wonder why anyone should be held guilty for unintentional sin, whether or not the wrongdoing is eventually brought to the offender's attention. The tendency of man is to absolve himself of any responsibility for misdeeds or sins beyond his control. But the sin offering does not give anyone the opportunity to disclaim responsibility for any wrong deeds, deliberate or unintentional. For deliberate or unintentional, a sin is still a sin. The reason a man commits evil is found in his nature. Because of his fallen nature, man will err even with the best of intentions. Genesis 3 and Romans 5:12–19 give us an account of man's fall, when he plunged himself and his posterity into the bonds of sin and mortality. Since the Fall man's nature is sinful, and that is what makes him do evil, intentionally or unintentionally. To offset man's disposition to sin, the sin offering taught the Israelite he could have an atonement for his sin nature. It is this offering also as a type that gives full meaning and substance to Christ's death, through which man can have a new life.

Various offerings

As with other offerings, a number of different kinds of animals could be offered as sin offerings. The priest who sinned brought a bull (4:3), the elders representing the congregation also offered a bull (4:15), the ruling authority provided a male goat (4:23), and the common people were permitted a variety of offerings: a female goat (4:28), a female lamb (4:32), two turtledoves or two young pigeons (5:7), or the tenth of an ephah of fine flour (5:11). The idea was to provide opportunity by God's grace for everyone to bring a sin offering according to his economic status. Provision was made even for the poorest person. He was allowed to offer flour, and even though it would be a bloodless offering, God in His mercy would accept it. It was not to be confused with the meal offering, however, and in its presentation by the priest no oil or incense was used.

The priests and the elders (representing the congregation) who sinned were to bring a bull, which was the most costly of offerings. Possibly the reason for this was that, insofar as the offending priest's sin was covered, it was especially bad because he was to be the example to his generation. Israel was a theocracy, and the priests were to be the leaders in spiritual things. If the priests went astray, the theocracy was on shaky ground, so the priests had greater responsibility. The ruler's responsibility was less than theirs, reflected in the less costly animal, a male goat, which he sacrificed.

Identification

The burnt offering taught the principle of identification. The sin offering also had the lesson of identification and demonstrated vividly that it was at the very heart of the whole sacrificial system. When the offerer laid his hands upon the animal, the animal took the place of the offerer and became his sin. The offerer then killed the animal, indicating that the penalty of sin is death. The animal took the offerer's penalty of death, and its life was given back to the offerer. That is the exchange-of-life principle.

If the Israelite really grasped this principle, he became a recipient of salvation, or of atonement for sin. It was not necessary for him to look forward to the Messiah's dying for sin, which was the fulfillment of the type. Very few actually caught the full figurative lesson of the sacrifices they made, although some must have realized that a validating sacrifice beyond the death of a mere animal, e.g., Isaiah 53:6, was implied. What was most important for the Israelite was that he appropriate the exchange of life when the sin-offering animal died. Aside from the remnant who became believers, however, the tragedy was that many merely seemed to have gone through the motions without catching the significance of the relation of the sacrifice to their own sin. And many today neither grasp nor desire salvation through the death of another, that is, Jesus.

Offering the blood

The requirement was that the offerer kill the animal, but it was the responsibility of an officiating priest to offer the blood. We already have pointed out that blood was the symbol of life and that in handling the blood, the ministering priest symbolically handled the life of the substitute. The blood of the substitute animal was symbolic of the new life to be given to the Israelite if he acted in faith to receive it.

1. *The priest who sinned.* The responsibility of the priest who sinned was heaviest. This can be seen in the way the blood of his sacrifice was applied. Some of the blood was taken into the tabernacle, and the officiating priest sprinkled it seven times in front of the veil separating the Holy Place and the Holy of Holies (v. 6). Actually this act was considered symbolic of applying the blood on the mercy seat inside the Holy of Holies. But since only the high priest could enter that area once a year on the Day of Atonement, the officiating priest on other occasions came as close to the veil and the mercy seat as he dared.

In addition the officiating priest put some blood on the horns of the altar of incense, which was in front of the veil, or curtain (v. 7), and the rest of the bull's blood was poured out at the base of the altar of burnt offering.

Notice the three key places where the blood was applied: the mercy seat, symbolizing atonement for sin; the altar of incense, symbolizing restoration of communion with God; and the altar of burnt offering, symbolizing renewal of dedication. It is the blood, as the symbol of a new life, which makes possible atonement, communion, and renewal.

2. *The congregation that committed error.* The same procedure was followed in the sacrifice for the sins of the congregation. The only difference was that the elders of the congregation laid their hands on the head of the bull instead of everyone doing it. That the same procedure was followed as with the priest who sinned indicates the gravity of congregational sin. And any individual's sin, if it implicated the whole congregation, was as grave as the sin of a priest. The elders acted on behalf of the congregation that erred. It was also their responsibility to ferret out the particular sin of the congregation. An officiating priest ministered on behalf of the elders.

3. *The civil authority who sinned.* In the sin offering for a civil ruler the application of the blood was different from the application of the previous offerings. No blood was brought into the tent of meeting;

rather, some of the blood was placed on the horns of the altar of burnt offering. The rest of the blood was poured at the base of this altar. Apparently the sin of a civil ruler was not as grave as that of a priest or that of the congregation. By no means does this minimize the sin of a civil authority; he had to bring his offering when he became aware of his sin. However, the priest's sin was treated more seriously than the ruler's because of the potential consequences of a religious leader's sin.

4. *Members of the general population who sinned.* In handling the blood for the general population, the officiating priest did the same thing as he did for a civil authority. He smeared some of the blood of the slain animal on the horns of the altar of burnt offering and poured the rest out at the base of the altar.

Disposal of the animals

After removing the blood from the sacrifice, the priest removed the fat and offered it up on the altar of burnt offering. After the offer of the animals on the altar, it was then necessary to care for their carcasses.

The bulls, because their blood had been taken into the tabernacle, were taken outside the camp and burned in a place where no ashes from other sacrifices were lying on the ground. Sin offerings were not to be confused with burnt offerings fired completely on the altar of burnt offerings. Neither were the ashes of the sin offering to be mingled with the remains of other offerings.

Animals other than bulls were handled differently. Their blood was *not* offered in the tent of meeting, and their flesh, except for the fat which was offered on the altar of burnt offering, became food for the priests (6:25–30). In offering one of two pigeons or turtledoves for the sin offering (5:7–9), the priest only nipped its head (instead of wringing off the head as in the burnt offering) and drained the blood, and then this bird possibly became food (Lev. 6:25–30). As for the flour, except for the handful offered on the altar, the rest was used as holy food for the priests.

Meaning

1. *To the Israelite.* The sin offering gave Israel a visual demonstration of the exchange-of-life principle. If the Israelite appropriated this truth by faith, his soul was redeemed from a fallen state. The people of Israel could know salvation and experience the new birth in a manner similar to that in which believers are redeemed today.

Let no one ever say that people in Old Testament days did not know what it meant to have sins forgiven. As we shall see in chapter 16, on the great Day of Atonement the Israelites could know that by means of the scapegoat their sins were removed from them forever. True, the redeemed Israelite continued to bring sin offerings even if he was saved, but he brought them with the perspective of a born-again person, with a testimony of what salvation meant. His offerings were in contrast to a person simply going through the steps of this offering without faith. Hopefully, through the testimony and life of redeemed Israelites, others would also be encouraged to believe. It is of primary importance to recognize the fact that the sin offering was the only means by which Israelites and others could enter into the circle of God's family; this was the first consideration—before there could be any dedication to do God's will. Man's way is to try to do good works in order to earn atonement. The sin offering, in its recorded form in Leviticus, reminds man that God's mercy provides redemption. But man, generally, then as now, does not want to be obligated to God; thus he spurns God's gift of life. Man's way and God's way clash, and in the end, if man does not accept God's offer, he will lose his soul.

2. *In type fulfillment.* The case for the type fulfillment by Jesus the Messiah actually commences with Old Testament application and is linked ultimately with New Testament validation. While most Israelites did not see beyond their own personal involvement in the sin offering, a few of the more spiritual ones certainly realized that there had to be some validating sacrifice behind all the sin offerings. Isaiah, for example, caught the type fulfillment in his prophecy: "And the LORD has laid on him the iniquity of us all" (53:6). The Messiah came into the world to bear our sins. The New Testament describes Jesus the Messiah as He stood on the Mount of Transfiguration talking with Moses and Elijah, and the subject of their conversation concerned His death (Luke 9:31). Jesus repeatedly warned His disciples that He was going to die. On one occasion (when Peter remonstrated with Him for saying He would die) Jesus rebuked Satan (Matt. 16:22–23). Satan had used Peter's lack of discernment to contest the express work Jesus had come to perform; even at this point we are permitted to see the great forces being built up for the struggle between Christ and Satan regarding redemption. In the Garden of Gethsemane Jesus struggled with the thought of taking the cup of sin, for which He would have to die; the trial was so intense that his sweat "was like drops of blood

falling to the ground" (Luke 22:44). On the cross He expressed with finality the type fulfillment for which He had come: "It is finished" (John 19:30). Like the animals of the sin offerings, He too died, shedding His blood. He died in this fashion because he *became* sin. It could not be otherwise. Death was the penalty for sin. So when Jesus took the sins of the world upon Himself at the cross, God's appointed altar, He had to die.

In addition, Jesus ministered as a priest, and the fulfillment of type followed that of the Levitical officiating priest's offering on behalf of another priest who had sinned. The blood on that occasion was taken into the tabernacle (or temple) and sprinkled in front of the veil. At that moment the priest was the closest he could come to the presence of God other than on the Day of Atonement. Jesus could act both as an officiating priest and as the sacrifice, offering His own blood as the symbol of His life in God's Holy Place on behalf of sinful man (Heb. 9:14). He, as the spotless, unblemished, and sinless Messiah, could act in the capacity of an officiating high priest and interpose His own blood for sinful souls in the presence of God.

Furthermore, the type also demonstrates, in the exchange-of-life principle, the way man can receive the life of Jesus through His death, as we shall discuss later.

There is even a type portrayal of the location where Jesus died. After the bull was offered on the altar, its carcass was taken outside the camp and burned in a clean place. Likewise, Christ's body hung on the cross outside the city (Heb. 13:12). The greatest respect and honor were given to such Old Testament atonement offerings, anticipating that Jesus would not suffer within the gates of the city. Our identification with Jesus also includes His reproach in having been treated as an outcast, a reproach we should gladly bear.

3. *To believers today.* What the Lord wanted Israelites to learn in the Old Testament regarding the exchange-of-life principle has not altered. However, since the Messiah's death the object in this exchange is now the Lord Himself. When we ask a person to receive Christ today, we ask him, in symbolic action, to place his hands on the head of Jesus. The person confesses his sins and believes that Jesus took them upon Himself on the cross. When Jesus did this, He became sin. The potential convert then believes that Christ died for him. The one believing on Jesus sees the shed blood of the Messiah as the symbol of His life, the receiving of which is made possible only because of His death.

This is not the end of the transaction. As Jesus takes away the sinful life of this person, He gives that one *His life,* effecting an exchange-of-life. We must emphasize that Jesus' life is not like that of any other. Because of who He is, His life has an unmatched quality. It is first of all eternal, and believers receive a gift that never ends. After leaving earth's mortal sphere, they will continue to live in the presence of the Father because the life of Jesus has been freely given to them. And in this life there is unmatched power that enables the believer to live triumphantly and victoriously. Apart from living in the power of this new life, Christians can never attain the standard which Christ expects; in fact, His standard is the life Jesus lived while He was here on earth. What mere human being is sufficient for this? No legalist can match the breadth of love and compassion Jesus had for sinners. No mere religion can enable one fully to attain to Christ's level of rendering good for evil, no matter what the circumstances. And no mere human love can be the ground of meaning for missionary activity. Strong in His superhuman love, Christians have carried the gospel to the four corners of the earth, enduring hardships, shame, suffering, and loss of life so that others can receive His love and peace in their souls. This power is available to all who receive His life in the exchange-of-life principle.

Lest this sound strange even to Christians, listen to Paul: "God made him who had no sin to be sin for us, so that in him we might become the righteousness of God" (2 Cor. 5:21). Because of this principle we can become part of the family of God, aside from performing dedicatory works. Here is the beginning of any relationship with God, and He makes it all possible through His grace and mercy.

Special sins

While up to this point there has been no mention of particular sins, it was the reminder of specific acts of sin which sharply pointed up the necessity of the sin offering.

Some of the specific sins which could be committed by members of the general population are mentioned in Leviticus (by no means an exhaustive list). There was the case of accidental ceremonial defilement (Lev. 5:2–3), which is described further in chapters 12–15, and the making of rash oaths on any occasion for good or for evil (5:4). In all of these cases, as soon as the Israelite saw his fault, he took the steps to atone for his sin.

He had to confess the wrong (v. 5) and bring the prescribed animal sacrifice specified for the lay person, a female goat or lamb (cf. 4:27, 32 and 5:7). As already indicated, if the Israelite was unable to bring a female goat or lamb for his sin offering, special concessions were made so that he could bring two turtledoves or two young pigeons (vv. 7–8). We see how these bird offerings served at least two purposes (vv. 7–9). One of the birds sufficed for the sin offering, but the other one served as the sacrifice for the burnt offering (v. 7; 1:14–17). God made it possible to offer most of the sacrifices in one approach, but He has a special relationship to and compassion for the poor. In God's permission for the special offerings by the poor, He wanted to be the "Portion" of the needy in a special way (Pss. 68:10; 69:33; 102:17; 113:7).

There were also circumstances in which a person was so poor he did not have the means for bringing even a pair of birds, already discussed previously (Lev. 5:11–13). It was possible for such a person to bring the tenth part of an ephah of fine flour, the recognized portion of each day's support, for the atonement for sin. This meant that in giving up his food for that day, a man fasted before the Lord.

E. The Law of the Guilt Offering (5:14–6:7)

Another "must" offering was the guilt, or trespass, offering for particular acts of sin. The law of Moses tied two concepts together to remind the worshiper that he had a double responsibility. Once the Israelite became aware of a particular sin he had committed, he first offered the appropriate sin offering, and afterwards, proceeded to offer a guilt offering.

Of the different kinds of sins in which a person could be involved, they may be divided into two groups—those against God and those against man. Leviticus treats both groups.

Description of two particular offenses

1. *Defrauding God.* Leviticus 5:15 refers to circumstances in which one treated the things of God deceitfully. This included injunctions concerning eating the first fruits (Exod. 34:26), shearing the first-born sheep (Deut. 15:19), etc. After offering the appropriate sin offering for his fraud, the Israelite then had to offer a ram without defect for a trespass offering. Furthermore, the ram had to be of a certain value in accordance with the standard of the sanctuary, reminding the offerer that a sin of this nature required a high penalty.

The actual handling of the animal offering is discussed in Leviticus 7:1–7.

In addition to the sacrifice of the animal the Israelite also had to learn that restitution was part of the penalty for sin. He was not only to replace what he had defrauded God of, but he was also to add to his restitution one-fifth of its value (5:16). If, for example, the Israelite did a dollar's worth of damage, he had to return not only the dollar but also another twenty cents. This extra fifth was given to the priest (the spiritual leader) since the offerer had committed an offense in God's things. Actually, the additional one-fifth represented a double tithe on top of the amount by which God was defrauded. Giving this additional one-fifth was an admission that God's rights had to be doubly acknowledged by a person when he attempted to defraud Him. With the offer of the animal and the restitution for the specific sin completed, the offender then was assured of atonement.

Similarly, there were other unspecified crimes in the things of worship that required atonement when an Israelite became aware of them (vv. 17, 18). The procedure was similar to that in verses 15, 16 except for the absence of restitution, since it was not possible to fix a price for damages.

2. *Sins against man* (6:1–7). The sins of this category relate to wrongs against the second table of the Law. It is interesting to note, however, that wrongs committed against man were also regarded as an affront to God. Before enumerating a partial list of sins directed against a fellow-man's interests, the writer states that such an offender "sins and is unfaithful to the LORD" (Lev. 6:1). To further underscore this concept, we see that in the English version of the Bible, 6:1–7 is attached to the end of chapter 5 in the Hebrew Bible, and thereby both sets of sins are combined. We need to know that any wrong perpetrated against man is also felt deeply by God Himself.

The Mosaic constitution dealt with a few of the legal aspects regarding the second part of the Decalogue, which pertains to man's sins against his fellow-man. Some specific sins of this sort were the following: a denial about something entrusted to him by a neighbor; appropriating something entrusted to him for himeslf; becoming involved in robbery; extorting a neighbor; or finding something that was lost and lying about the rightful owner so as to appropriate it for himself. If a thief could be found, he had to be prosecuted (Exod. 22:7–9); otherwise, when a person's conscience convicted him of sin, he was to take steps to confess it, make restitution, and then seek atonement (Lev. 6:4–7).

The guilty person restored in full the principal he took. But in addition he added one-fifth of the value of the principal, just as in the case when holy things were withheld from God. The penalty here was also a double tithe, a double acknowledgment of the owner's right to the article entrusted, of which he had been unjustly deprived (v. 5). Again, such wrongdoing was regarded as sin against the Lord (v. 2), for God sought to maintain the rights of men with strict justice in accordance with His holy character. To steal from another violates His standards.

The offending party also had to atone for his sin with a ram of a specific worth reckoned in shekels (5:15; 6:6), the shekel being fixed by the religious leaders in accordance with the accepted weight and current value of the metals. Here the trespass offering differed from the sin offering. With the latter, provision was made for a variety of animals in accordance with the offerer's position in responsibility as well as in his economic means; in the trespass offering, however, everyone brought the same animal, a ram of a fixed worth. This offering by every offender was a reminder that restitution had to be made to God as well as to man when a man defrauded his fellowman. But note the order: first, restitution was made to the person who had suffered loss, and second, God's honor was vindicated in the sacrifice of the ram. The manner in which the animal was sacrificed is described in 7:1–7. After the offer of the ram and the payment of restitution (6:5), the offender was pardoned by the Lord (v. 7).

Meaning

1. *Fulfillment of the type.* Just as Jesus Christ is the fulfillment in type of the sin offering, so is He the fulfillment in type of the trespass offering. The main features of the trespass offering were the double tithe in restitution and the worth of the ram for the sacrifice.

Isaiah the prophet caught the significance of the guilt or trespass offering in Isaiah 53:10, where he says: "The Lord makes his life a guilt offering." The word for offering in that verse is the same word used for guilt offering in Leviticus 5:14–6:7. While the prophet pictured the death of Jesus as a sin offering (Isaiah 53:6), he also portrayed the death of Jesus as a trespass offering (v. 10).

One aspect in type of the restitution is that as an expensive twofold restitution was made by the Israelite in the procedure of rectifying his deeds, so there had to be One who alone could effect the ultimate restoration of all the honor God's law had suffered through man's sins and frauds. Only Jesus was worthy to complete this task. Jesus alone is without sin, and only His life, as He offered Himself a sacrifice, could suffice to pay for the damage sinful man has wrought against God and other men.

As for the ram, it was of a certain monetary value in shekels, and this fact also pointed to a specific fulfillment in type. The ram was not just any ram but was of a kind representing one of the most costly breeds in the country, known as "the choice rams of Bashan" (Deut. 32:14). In type Jesus fulfilled such an offering, and the focus now is upon the costliness of Jesus *as the offering.* Peter underscored the price paid by the Messiah, "the precious blood of Christ" (1 Peter 1:19), indicating that forgiveness was costly. It is the death of Jesus that makes possible full restitution to God for each person's offenses, and therefore, full restoration for the offender.

2. *To believers today.* Restitution applies to believers today as well. When a Christian is convicted of a particular sin, he should not only replace what he has taken from God or from man, but as far as possible he should provide more than he stole. Believers today should heed carefully the good advice of wisdom: "Fools mock at making amends for sin, but good will is found among the upright" (Prov. 14:9). No one should mock at the confession of and restitution for sins against God or man. When we transgress against God and rob Him of money, time, or talents, which are to be used for Him, should not our consciences be awakened? And should we not repay and make restitution before and to God? This also applies to any wrongs committed against our fellow-man. Should we do less today, now that Christ has come, than what the Old Testament saint did as he lived within the framework of the Mosaic constitution? By no means! What we wrongfully take from God or from man, we must return or restore, insofar as it is possible, before we enter into worship as believers.

The lesson of the trespass offering has its application for unbelievers today as well. Besides the lesson the sin offering has for the nature of sin, the recognition of particular sins is something that cannot be overlooked. First of all, it is the conviction of specific sins that emphasizes the necessity for salvation, as seen earlier in the sin offering section. It is the work of the Holy Spirit to convict men of sin (John

16:8) and to bring conscience-stricken people, in their specific crimes either against their fellow-man or against God, to receive Christ's life in the exchange-of-life principle. Second, there is the recognition that Christ's death was for individual sins as well. "Christ died for our sins" (1 Cor. 15:3) is a reminder of the response we should have to the great lessons of the trespass offering.

For Further Study

1. In a Bible dictionary or encyclopedia (see bibliography) read articles on: blood, dedication, sacrifice (offerings), salvation, tabernacle (temple).

2. After reviewing the procedure for the forgiveness of sin and its meaning to the Israelite and believers today, outline the steps to present the plan of salvation. Then try using this presentation with the next contact God gives you.

3. Do you think that the payment of restitution which accompanied the guilt offering would be a testimony to the nonbeliever?

4. Do you think that the lessons of the two dedication offerings (burnt and meal) relate to the Christian's work ethic in his place of employment?

5. Take a concordance and look up the word "peace" in the letters of Paul. Do you suppose Paul had reason to be thankful at the Lord's Table in view of what he said about "peace"?

Chapter 2

Law of the Offerings—
Regulations for the Priests
(Leviticus 6:8–7:30)

In contrast to the first five chapters in which Moses presents the individuals' part in the offerings, he now provides supplemental directions for the priests' ministry in connection with the offerings.

A. Burnt Offering (6:8–13)

The fire

One of the functions of the officiating priest was to make sure that the fire on the altar of burnt offering never went out. This fire, originally kindled by God (Lev. 9:24), emphasized a divinely prescribed order of worship and the centrality of the altar. Ever after, the priests kept the fire going, cautiously preserving the heated coals while the Israelites were on the march in the desert and also carefully sustaining the same fire in their permanent settlement in the land of Israel. Day or night the priests never permitted the divinely given fire to go out, and this became a reminder to Israel that God neither slumbers nor sleeps (vv. 9, 12, 13).

The fire consumed the burnt offering, and as we have already seen in the consideration of this offering, it represented the Israelite who brought it. But the Israelite did not dedicate his life to God nor lay his life down as some mere human act. It took both man's willingness and God's acceptance to complete the transaction of dedication. Through the fire the priests began, God signified His acceptance of a life given up to Him.

The memorial portion of the meal offering was also consumed by the fire on the altar, as well as the fat of the peace offerings and the appropriate portions of the sin and trespass offerings. In the sin and trespass offerings, the fire was a solemn reminder of God's judgment upon sin. Regardless of Old Testament or New Covenant dispensations, the figure of God as fire persists: "For our God is a consuming fire" (Heb. 12:29). Likewise, one should not forget the ministry of the Messiah in type. When He died as the sin and trespass offerings, eternal flames fed upon our Substitute and the sin which He bore on our behalf. The death of the Messiah in this manner becomes a solemn warning to anyone who dies in his sins without His atonement; indeed, the Lord "is patient with you, not wanting anyone to perish, but everyone to come to repentance" (2 Peter 3:9).

The national offerings

Two burnt offerings are mentioned—the night offering (v. 9) and the morning offering (v. 12). These were national dedicatory offerings prescribed in the law, one lamb to be offered in the morning (around 6:00 A.M.) and the other lamb to be offered "between the evenings" (probably around 3:00 P.M., Exod. 29:38–42). Just as individuals offered burnt offerings, so did the nation. Israel was to be holy and totally dedicated to God because of her covenant, as demonstrated by her two national offerings on each day. The evening burnt offering was kept on the altar until morning with the fire burning (v. 9), and the offering for the day remained burning there during the whole day (v. 12), as a constant reminder of a nation and its people dedicated to God's holy purposes.

Priests' clothes

The holy and beautiful garments of the high priest had rich meaning (Exod. 28), and even the clothes of the priests were to remind them of their special ministry. Their linen robes, as well as the prescribed linen undergarments next to the skin, were regarded as marks of purity (Lev. 6:10; Exod. 28:42, 43). In the ministry no clothes were worn that would induce perspiration, e.g., wool, because even perspiration suggested uncleanness, and the priests washed often in order to be ceremonially clean. In the service in the Holy Place linen was less likely to induce perspiration and cause undue uncleanliness. In time linen came to be regarded as the symbol of purity and of righteous deeds. The church as the bride of Christ at the marriage supper of the Lamb will be clothed in fine linen, bright and clean; we are told specifically that the fine linen is the righteous acts of the believers (Rev. 19:8).

The ashes

As the priest ministered, one of his tasks was to take the ashes and put them beside the altar. It was necessary to keep the fire on the altar clean and bright for the various fresh sacrifices. The ashes beside the altar were a reminder of a finished sacrifice offered by an Israelite or of one offered on behalf of the nation.

When the priest had cleared the altar of the ashes, he changed to ordinary clothes and carried the ashes outside the camp to a clean place (Lev. 6:11). These ashes were memorials of the animal sacrifices and considered to be holy and separate, still belonging to God. In the days of the temple the ashes were deposited in a consecrated area south of the city, and for this reason no one lived there.

It is prophetically significant that when Joseph of Arimathea claimed the body of Jesus (John 19:38), he hastily prepared it for burial (since the Sabbath was coming) and then laid it in a *new* tomb, a tomb ". . . in which no one had ever been laid" (John 19:41). The Messiah's body was laid to rest in a clean place, even as the ashes of the burnt offering sacrifices were carried to a clean place (see also Lev. 4:12, 21). The burial of Jesus was a providential arrangement!

B. Grain Offering (6:14–18)

As we have already seen in Leviticus 2, the memorial portion of the grain (or meal) offering was offered to the Lord, while the remainder became food for the priests (6:15–16). In this way God took care of His own servants. The grain was to be eaten as unleavened cakes, and no leaven—which would intimate sin or corruption (v. 17)—was to be added. The food from the sacrifice, including unleavened bread, was prepared and eaten in the courtyard around the tent of meeting (or temple), an area restricted to the use of the priests. There was a circle of deep awe around the altar and its offerings, but life for the priests also had its joys that could be shared around the tables where the food was eaten.

C. Grain Offering When High Priests Were Consecrated (6:19–23)

When high priests were consecrated to their office, there were special grain offerings. When Aaron and his sons were anointed, they brought the specified grain offering, which was the tenth of an ephah (or an omer, i.e., two dry quarts) of flour. Perhaps this amount was based on the omer of manna placed before the Lord and kept throughout the generations (Exod. 16:33); this omer of manna was a reminder that God would sustain His people. Therefore, the grain offering by the new high priest was his memorial meal offering. It appears also that the high priest continued to offer this offering for the entire term of his office, "a regular (perpetual) grain offering" (v. 20).

The meal was to be of fine flour (Lev. 6:20) and was to be prepared with oil on a griddle (v. 21). Since the priests had no inheritance of land, they could procure fine flour from one who did have. The priests did expend some effort in preparing these cakes (vv. 21–22). The ministering priest placed these cakes on the altar to be burned in their entirety (vv. 22–23); they were not eaten because they were a priest's offering (v. 23). As we shall see in Leviticus 8–9, this offering, burned completely by the priest, was a type of the Messiah, who as a unique High Priest offered Himself completely.

D. Sin Offering (6:24–30)

Here is a reminder again that the sin offering of Leviticus was regarded with reverence as being most holy. In the exchange-of-life principle one could have his sin forgiven on the altar of God (ch. 4). In type we remember the act by which the Messiah took our sins and gave us the most holy gift of life.

While the offering was regarded as holy, yet in grace and mercy God provided the flesh of the offered animals as food for His priests, who served at the altar (vv. 24, 29). To stress the sanctity of this special food, however, God stated that the priests could eat it only in a place set apart from the laity, i.e., in the courtyard of the tent of meeting. The very eating of this meat set the priests apart from the common people. Partaking of this food reminded the priests of God's holiness and of their need to be holy (vv. 26, 27). Heinous indeed was the situation in which the priests fed on the sin offerings of the people and then turned around and practiced iniquity (Hos. 4:8). God did not want the ritual to degenerate into occasions to sin. Neither does He today desire that we have holy processions, meetings, and solemn occasions in churches where the cross is held up but where people only turn back to their sins, thereby desecrating Jesus' death.

To further impress upon the priests the holy character of the food, God added a number of warnings. If any of the blood of the animal flesh splashed onto a garment, the garment was to be washed in a holy place; it was not to be taken out among the people. In this way the blood, as the symbol of a new life, was to be regarded as sacred and was not to be desecrated; the shedding of this blood was made possible only because of the death of an animal as a sacrifice for sin. In type we also regard the blood of Jesus as sacred, for by it we have eternal life; its benefits too were made available to men because of His death for sinful man (see again the emphasis on the "exchange-of-life" principle, Lev. 4).

Another warning concerned the cooked meat juices of the animal flesh. The kind of pot in which the meat was boiled made a difference. If it was prepared in an earthenware vessel, this vessel was broken after its use because there was no way the pot could be cleansed; the meat juices penetrated into the very core of the earthenware. Rather than contaminate these meat juices either by letting them become stale in the pot after its use (thereby breaking the law concerning old meat) or by mixing these meat juices with some other food (thereby defiling the sin offering since it was holy and separate), the priests broke the pot. On the other hand, if the meat was cooked in a more expensive bronze vessel, which did not absorb the food, it was necessary only to scour the pot thoroughly. The sacredness and holiness of the animal sin offering was therefore preserved and emphasized.

The final warning was that no flesh of any sin offering was to be eaten if its blood was offered *inside* the tent of meeting or the temple (ch. 4:6, 17). Such sin offerings were those on behalf of erring priests or those in which sin was chargeable to the congregation. Possibly because of the special holiness of these offerings, they prefigure in its entirety the Savior's death. He suffered and died outside the camp, the innocent for the guilty (Heb. 13:12). Therefore, while God in His mercy provided food from some of the sin offerings, He wanted to clarify what the sin offering meant in terms of atonement. One good way to emphasize the importance of the sin offering in its relation to the death of the Messiah was to prohibit the eating of the food of the sin offering on behalf of the most responsible groups of people in Old Testament society.

Both the priest and the lay person under the Law could know what God's grace meant, and many did accept new life, whether they fully understood the type or not. Today, a person has no excuse; not only does he have the object lesson of the Old Testament sin offering, but he can also recognize the New Testament description of Christ's death as our sin offering, granting us a new and an eternal life.

E. Guilt Offering (7:1–7)

Further details regarding the guilt (or trespass) offering, previously referred to in Leviticus 5:14–6:7, now appear.

Once again we find the reminder of the necessity of the slaying of the animal by the offerer, portraying the penalty paid for specific sins. When the animal died, the priest took the blood and sprinkled it around on the altar (v. 2). Again, the application of the blood was to remind the erring sinner of his guilt; of a specific, broken law; and of payment of the penalty by a substitute.

Repetition was beneficial in the sacrificial system, and God did not weary of repeating the procedures for handling the guilt offering. The Lord had in mind the sinners who would come before Him as well as the Levitical priests who would have to officiate. God was patient and long-suffering so that His people would learn and eventually appropriate the lessons of these offerings. God's love is without measure so that men might know Him!

After the animal was cut up, the priest took the fat portions (vv. 3–5) and placed them on the altar for an offering made by fire. The fat, as we have already discussed, represented God's bounty and blessing and was offered back to God. In type we also see the Messiah offered, paying the penalty for *every* particular sin.

The rest of the animal served as food for the priests (v. 6), who had no inheritance in the land. So the Lord was their portion and inheritance (Josh. 18:7). This flesh also was to be eaten in a holy place, i.e., the courtyard of the tent of meeting (or temple).

F. Special Provisions for the Priests (7:8–10)

In a further gesture of His bounty God stipulated that when a bull was presented as a burnt offering (v. 8 refers to a rich man's offering), the officiating priest could keep the skin of the bull. This hide, sold to a tannery for leather goods, would bring some means of financial support to the priest who had served on that occasion. As the priests ministered on behalf of other offerings, they had food from these offerings, e.g., the meat of the sin and trespass offerings. They also could have the various grain offerings that were left after the presentation of the portion for the memorials (vv. 9, 10).

When the people were faithless in their relation with the Lord, the priests suffered. On the other hand, when the people were right with God and brought their offerings to Him, the priests rejoiced.

Through these occasions the situation of the priests determined the spiritual status of the nation. When they had their share, they could assume that the people's relationship with God was good. When the priests lacked because of the people's apathy in worship, the priests were to call the nation to repentance. When the nation refused to listen, the Lord brought famine on the land, causing the priests even more hardship. Periods of drought and famine were serious because grain and animals that could have been offered only died. This should have served as an occasion for the priests to call the nation back to God. Tragically, many of the priests failed in this task and became apostate themselves. God called the prophets to be special servants to preach to the nation. This will be discussed in detail when we study chapter 26.

G. The Peace Offering (7:11, 28–34)

The occasion and reason for partaking of peace offerings (flesh and the unleavened and leavened breads) have already been presented in the material of Leviticus 3, and for part of this chapter as well (7:12–18). It remains here only to discuss the priest's participation in the peace offering. Perhaps the instructions about breads and the use of peace offerings and of vow, or freewill, offerings might seem tedious. But Israel was carefully guided as to the proper approach in her worship of the God of truth and love, and she was instructed in the types of the coming Messiah.

In the priest's association with the peace offerings (vv. 28–34) there is further evidence of God's care for His servants. While we have already noted that the offerer made his offering the occasion of a festive meal (actually of the Table of God), it would have been inconceivable to have feasted on this flesh without having given opportunity for God's priests to feast also. God, as the Host of this banquet, saw to it that the priesthood had a share.

When presenting a peace sacrifice, an offerer killed the animal, and the priest then took the blood and sprinkled it around the altar. But as the sacrificial animal was dressed, the offerer gave the fat and the breast to the officiating priest as an offering to the Lord (v. 30). The fat portion was placed on the altar, but the breast belonged to all the priests after it had been waved. This waving ceremony was a beautiful sight; as the offerer held the flesh in his hands, the officiating priest put his hands underneath the hands of the offerer and moved hands and breast toward the altar and then away from it in a horizontal motion.

The words "with his own hands" described the voluntary nature of the sacrifice offer to God by the Israelite. In turn the priests were reminded that it was God who made all blessings possible when He provided food for His servants.

In addition the right thigh of the offering was presented to God as a contribution or a heave offering (vv. 32, 33) inasmuch as it was lifted off from the animal in an up-and-down motion while facing the altar. This portion was considered as offered to God but according to His instructions it was to be given to the officiating priest for his own festal meal. The priests, during their festal meal, could thank God for a generous people who had brought the peace offerings. These were God's directives in caring for His priests (v. 34), and the people were to be obedient to His will.

As the Israelites ate peace offerings at a table where God was considered to be the Host, so the priests who ate from portions of the peace offerings also understood God to be their gracious Host. The priests who were spiritually minded realized that they were partaking of His grace and bounty. As they ate of this food, a few also saw the Messiah as their peace and the One responsible for their blessings.

The principle of God's providing for His priests transcends dispensations. Do not God's people today bring of their tithes and offerings to Him? And can we not regard a portion of them as God's unique peace offering of affection and power given to ministers so that they may live and serve? Accordingly, should not those who determine what is given to these special servants of God do it in such a way that the servants will have cause to glorify God for His goodness and will also sense the love and affection of God's people?

H. Miscellaneous Instructions (7:19–27)

In the complex rules concerning the peace offering some basic instruction was necessary since so many rules were involved. Any flesh of the peace offerings that touched anything unclean was not to be eaten (v. 19). Only people ceremonially clean could eat these sacrifices. As for the people who would partake of the sacrificial meal, we need to remember that the peace offering was the last in the round of sacrifices and that the priests who officiated could eventually detect persons who were not ceremonially clean. There were also ways to check animals that were not proper and fit as offerings. In these ways God's law carefully designated who could sit at His table for a peace offering feast and what could be placed on the table. Care also was necessary so as not to despoil the meaning of the Messiah antitype, who was the very fulfillment of peace.

To countermand God's Word in any way as to the peace offering, i.e., to be ceremonially unclean while eating the sacrifices or to be unclean by touching any forbidden thing before eating, brought a severe condemnation (vv. 20, 21). A person who disobeyed God in such ways was to be cut off, i.e., no longer associated with the covenant people. This was tantamount to leaving that person to the judgment of God; there was no sacrifice to atone for such a sin, and if this person was to be restored to the people of Israel, it would have to be by an act of God's mercy. This would be rare, since flouting the law of the peace offering was serious indeed; proper worship of and honor given to God were to be carefully observed.

To be "cut off from his people" could very well mean immediate death (22:9). Lest the reader think this was harsh treatment under the Law and that things are easier under grace, let him ponder carefully 1 Corinthians 11:30–32, which also indicates untimely death as punishment for unwarranted sin. Of course, part of God's training in holy living is to make the believer more and more sensitive to sin, to draw him away from it, and to bring him nearer to God so that he may learn that God is exceedingly merciful.

Further injunctions concern eating fat (vv. 23–25). There are many uses of the word "fat," and one symbolic meaning is "rich" or "the best." Two examples are the following: Asher's bread was to be fat (Gen. 49:20) and the land of the Canaanites was called a fat land (Neh. 9:24–25). But in the verses under consideration the word fat is actually a literal reference to the fat of an animal to be offered. The reason the law explicitly forbade eating fat was because the fat that was burned in the fire on the altar was actually representative of a gift offered to God and sanctified by Him. To have eaten the fat would have been taking from God what belonged to Him. Fat was also a reminder of God's blessings, which were to be offered back to Him in thanksgiving. Some fat could, however, be put to domestic use, e.g., that obtained from any animal which had died from natural causes or through violence (Lev. 7:24).

The warning is repeated in verse 25 and is directed primarily to the priests, since it was their task to offer all the fat of such an offering on the altar before partaking of whatever was available to them. In the case of a peace offering the officiating priest also was to make sure that all the fat was removed from what was given back to the offerer for his feast. When the priests were remiss in their ministry, either by being careless or by actually being in an apostate condition, they were held responsible for the offerer's fault if the latter didn't know better. When either a priest or a lay person violated this law about eating the fat of sacrificial animals, he was to be cut off from the people. This was a warning again to listen, learn, and do the holy will of God. To this day, traditional Jews refrain from eating any kind of fat.

An equally serious injunction was that under no circumstance was anyone to eat blood from any living thing (vv. 26, 27). It has already been mentioned that blood and life are synonymous (to be discussed further in ch. 17), and the reader has already seen that the blood of the sacrificial animals was applied on or about the altar in various offerings for sin, trespasses, dedication, and thanksgiving. It would be unthinkable to use blood for any other purpose than these mentioned. And, of course, how could anyone despise the Messiah antitype by misusing the blood in what was involved in the type? For anyone to have eaten blood in any form would only have invited the judgment of God, for "that person must be cut off from his people" (v. 27).

I. Conclusion (7:28–38)

This is not only the conclusion to the consideration of the law of the offerings in its regulations for the priests but also for those regulations relating to individuals. From now on no explanation will be provided for these offerings in various circumstances, but the reader should keep in mind procedures relative to the offerings discussed above, as those procedures impart new and richer meanings in various applications.

Aaron and his sons, and after them all the priests consecrated to their tasks (v. 35), had the high privilege of ministering holy things presented to the Lord. Yes, it was their duty to represent Israel in the presence of God in His tabernacle (later the temple). For their tasks young priests had careful training, which culminated in their ordination offering when they were consecrated (v. 36). They then had a lifelong ministry. This order of priesthood continued for as long as the Mosaic constitution was in force. Priests also had the ministry of teaching successive generations of Israelites how to present their various offerings. The Law served as a schoolmaster for both priest and lay person, teaching them how they could enter into a salvation experience. Eventually the nation was to be led to acknowledge the Messiah antitype of whom the offerings and ministries of priests so richly spoke. When the Messiah did appear, there were all the means by which His credentials could be determined. The law of the offerings should also enrich *our* understanding of the life and work of Jesus Christ.

For Further Study

1. In a Bible dictionary or encyclopedia (see bibliography) read articles on: Aaron, altar, ashes, Levites, priest(hood), priest's dress.

2. What is the point where people were to realize that offerings were brought to the Lord and not to the priests? Is this a good lesson for believers today?

3. In at least two of the Bible encyclopedias, make a list of how "fire" is used whenever it relates to the altar in worship and sacrifice.

4. Many times the priests who officiated were not believers and disregarded both blood and food of the sin offerings. Did this mean that when such a priest ministered, a sincere Israelite could not become a believer when he presented his offerings?

5. Was it possible for people and priests to become legalistic when performing all the many demands of the worship system? On the other hand, could genuine believers among people and priests perform joyously all the functions of worship? Any lessons for today?

Chapter 3

Laws of Priestly Regulations
(Leviticus 8:1–10:20)

The passage "Day after day every priest stands and performs his religious duties" (Heb. 10:11) reminds us of the function of the priesthood. Levi was cursed by Jacob, and therefore this tribe could not have any inheritance rights in the land of Israel (Gen. 49:7). Yet because the Levites stood with Moses in the rebellion (Exod. 32:26–29), God's mercy was extended to them so that they were chosen to assist the priests (Num. 3:5–6). Their inheritance consisted of the altar and the holy things (Josh. 18:7). But the Levitical priesthood ended when the never-ending priesthood of the Messiah began. We also need to appreciate, from a number of applications, the practical guidance given to us as believers who are functioning as priests now (1 Peter 2:9). Leviticus 8–10 discusses the way the Levitical priests were set apart for God's service, in explanation of Exodus 28:41 and 29:1.

A. Consecration of Aaron and His Sons (8:1–36)

The calling and cleansing

The first procedure of consecration was performed by Moses on behalf of Aaron and his immediate four sons. Thereafter, an officiating priest performed this procedure for every new priest who came of age, i.e., thirty years old. To prepare for the first consecration, Moses instructed Aaron to bring the proper offerings (vv. 1–5), and the congregation assembled to view the consecration of the priesthood (v. 3).

The consecration began when Moses washed Aaron and his sons with the water from the laver at the tent doorway, stressing the fact that purification was necessary if one was to approach a holy God (v. 6). This act was symbolic of inner cleansing as well.

Aaron's clothing

Moses next invested Aaron with the clothes that represented the high priest's office (vv. 7–9). The tunic, a long garment that was worn next to the person, was made of fine linen (Exod. 28:39). Aaron also wore linen undergarments, under the tunic, undergarments that covered the body from the waist to the thigh (Exod. 28:42). The fine linen was symbolic of personal righteousness (Rev. 19:8).

Aaron was then clothed with the robe of the ephod (Exod. 28:31–35), a long, seamless garment of blue linen. It had an opening for the head and was worn over the tunic. On the hem of the robe pomegranates (the symbol of fruitfulness) were embroidered in blue, purple, and scarlet; hemmed alternately with the pomgranates were gold bells (the symbol of testimony) that sounded as the high priest moved about in his service in the sanctuary. A sash girded the robe.

Aaron then put on the ephod itself, a short, outer garment similar to a jacket (Exod. 28:6–30, 39). It is described as having been made of blue, purple, and scarlet material and of finely twisted linen (Exod. 28:6); it was made of two pieces—one in the front and one in the back—which were united by two shoulder pieces and by an artistic band around the bottom. The ephod had the singular characteristic of being worn only by one occupying the high priestly office. It was this article of clothing by which the prophet proclaimed that Israel would be without a priest for many days (Hos. 3:4–5).

On the shoulders of the ephod were two onyx stones, set in gold and engraved with the names of the twelve tribes of Israel, six on each stone (Exod. 28:7–12, 27). Aaron bore these tribal names as a memorial as he represented Israel before the Lord. The breastplate was then placed on Aaron's chest and fastened to the shoulder pieces of the ephod with golden chains. The plate was formed in a square, and it had a gold setting mounted on it containing twelve precious stones; there were four rows with three stones in each row. Also mounted on the breastplate was evidently some kind of fold or pouch which contained the Urim and Thummim (Exod. 28:15–21, 29–30), used in some way to ascertain the Lord's will (Num. 27:21; 1 Sam. 28:6; Ezra 2:63). The breatplate with the names of the tribes of Israel was worn over the heart as the high priest carried the rights of the sons of Israel before the Lord (Exod. 28:30). This was symbolic of the high priest's care and love for his people and also of the pledge that he would intercede for them. Jesus also acts in this capacity! After offering Himself in the atonement, He now bears our names on His heart as He intercedes for us before God (Heb. 7:25; 1 John 2:1). But there is also an application for us in our function as believer-priests, when we pray for each other.

Moses also placed a turban of fine linen (Exod. 28:37) on Aaron's head, and on the front of the turban he placed a golden plate, engraved "HOLY TO THE LORD" (Exod. 28:36), a constant reminder of the person of the high priest. He was set apart for the holy things of God, and his thoughts and deeds were to be righteous. In the teaching of the type concerning the Messiah as our High Priest, He made atonement for us and now ever intercedes for us, providing the mercy and grace of God freely, but in accordance with the holiness of the Lord. Holiness is the very essence of God and is what guarantees the outpouring of His love, grace, and mercy.

Anointing

Moses took the anointing oil (symbol of the Holy Spirit) and anointed the tabernacle and all that was in it before it was used (vv. 10, 11) by sprinkling the oil over everything, thereby setting it all apart to the service of God. The altar of burnt offering was sprinkled seven times as if to perfectly anoint the place where God would meet with His people.

Aaron himself was next anointed, or set apart, for his office before he could even minister (v. 12). Therefore Moses, acting for God, anointed Aaron (poured the oil on Aaron's head) before the sacrifices were slain, although Aaron's sons were not anointed with oil until the proper application of the blood had been made (v. 30). The high priest was set apart, distinctive from the rest, with the "precious oil poured on the head" (Ps. 133:2). Christ as our High Priest is also set apart in a special way: "Therefore God, your God, has set you above your companions by anointing you with the oil of joy" (Heb. 1:9).

Priest's clothing

Aaron's sons were now clothed in their priestly dress. They wore their tunics tied with sashes and also wore their headbands (Lev. 8:13). They were not clothed as Aaron was because they had to respect him who alone had the right to enter the Holy of Holies. This is the picture of us today as believer-priests, serving God and His Christ, the great High Priest.

The sacrifices

Various sacrifices were used in the consecration of priests. The first was the bull of the sin offering, with which Aaron and his sons were identified by placing their hands upon the head of the animal (v. 14). When the bull was killed, Moses took the blood and put some of it on the horns of the altar to purify it and then poured the rest at the altar's base. Note here how closely intertwined was the atonement for the sins of the priests and the purification of the places where the priests ministered; the sins of the priests were regarded as defiling the altar and the holy things. Both priests and holy places were cleansed by the blood from the animal substitute; since life was considered as being "in the blood" (Lev. 17:11), God actually viewed the life of the substitute sacrifice as being interposed between defiled priests and places and Himself. The rest of the ritual of the sin offering on behalf of the priests then took place (described in ch. 4).

Moses then presented to Aaron and his sons the ram of the burnt offering, and again Aaron and his sons identified with it (v. 18). Note here that Moses did not bring the most expensive offering nor the poorest one but rather the middle-class presentation, suggestive of what priests should bring in the future when they wanted to offer a dedicatory sacrifice. The offering was made in the prescribed manner, emphasizing particularly the dedication of the priests (vv. 19–21).

A distinctive ram for the ordination of Aaron and his sons was then brought by Moses, and again there was the usual identification with this animal (v. 22). Moses slaughtered this animal, and since this sacrifice served in a consecrative sense, Moses took some of the animal's blood and placed it on the priests' right ears, right thumbs, and right toes (vv. 23–24), starting first with Aaron. Symbolically, this was to signify that the ears (a call for proper hearing and obedience), the thumbs (an appeal for approved service), and the toes (a call for a perfect walk) were especially set apart to God. The blood (or life) of consecration was a dramatic lesson to newly consecrated priests that the quality of their ministry did matter. Since the priests had identified with this animal, its blood was the symbol of their new lives dedicated to God in every part. Concerning the Messiah antitype as He fulfilled the consecration aspect, we see Him in total dedication to His Father in His ministry as High Priest.

In a peculiar way the rest of this ordination offering was handled as a thanksgiving offering. The fat, certain inner parts, and the right thigh of the consecration animal were gathered together by Moses (v. 25), along with one unleavened cake, one oiled cake, and one wafer (the memorial portion of the meal offering). He placed the cakes and wafer on the fat and on the right thigh of the sacrificial animal. All were now put into the hands of Aaron and his sons in succession, and each, prompted by Moses, offered the portions as wave offerings (vv. 26–27). It was as if the priests had offered these pieces, but yet they could not actually put them on the altar since they were not fully installed as priests. Moses himself then offered the proper portions on the altar for the priests as their thanksgiving offering to God (v. 28). It was a high honor to be installed as a priest, and the portions were presented to God in thanksgiving. Since Moses officiated while there were no bona fide priests as yet, he kept the breast for his personal food (v. 29; 7:31).

Further anointing (v. 30)

As already stated, the regular priests were not anointed until after the sacrificial animals had been offered on their behalf. This anointing in verse 30 was different from the previous one. In the previous anointing Aaron alone had been singled out (as every high priest thereafter), but here Moses, after mixing some of the oil that had already been used with some of the remaining blood of the ram of ordination, sprinkled Aaron and his sons and their garments, thereby consecrating the priests and their clothes (Exod. 29:21). The priests could not function until the atonement had been effected and the dedication blood for full consecration had been provided, symbolic of a new life totally dedicated to God. One might reflect that the dedication procedures of the priests of the Mosaic constitution appear very detailed. But we today who are believer-priests should remind ourselves that dedication to God under the New Covenant is just as meticulous. Every detail of our lives and service is to be unspotted by the world; i.e., our garments are not to be polluted (Jude 23) or soiled (Rev. 3:4).

Thanksgiving

With the rest of the flesh of the ordination sacrifice Aaron and his sons were instructed to make a thanksgiving meal (v. 31). The meat was boiled in the courtyard before the tent (the fire being obtained from the altar), and the newly installed priests sat, in a sense, at the table of God to thank Him for the new ministry on which they were to embark. There was also the bread of the grain offering to remind them of the sanctity of their new priestly labor. This is indeed a reminder of the Messiah's ministry as a priest on our behalf. Our service as believer-priests is a joy, as well, and we have every reason to be thankful.

Seclusion

Aaron and his sons were not to leave the courtyard of the tent of meeting but were to remain at the entrance for seven days and nights (vv. 33–35). The priests were being prepared for their office after atonement and consecration had been made. Possibly the seven days also provided time to ascertain if there were any blemishes in any one of the priests, thus invalidating him for his office (see chs. 13 and 14). The seven days and nights would most certainly provide time for the priests to meditate on the lessons of their new ministry in the things which the Lord had commanded.

B. Installation of the Priests (9:1–24)

The consecration of the priests was now completed, and Aaron and his sons were ready to be installed. Moses instructed Aaron and his sons to procure animals for offerings for themselves (v. 2). He also told the elders of the congregation to bring their appropriate offerings and to draw near to the front of the tent of meeting (vv. 3–5). After everyone had assembled, Moses indicated that Aaron should proceed, first to offer the sacrifices for himself and his sons, and then to minister on behalf of the congregation (v. 7). After this the priests were properly installed, and the glory of God appeared to approve all that had transpired (v. 6).

Priest's offerings (vv. 8–14)

Aaron began with the sin offering to make atonement for himself and his sons (v. 8) which was necessary before he could publicly minister. After this was completed and Aaron had slaughtered the calf, his sons presented the blood to him, who then applied it to the horns of the altar. The rest of the ritual of the atonement offering went as prescribed. We see in a unique way how Aaron's sons helped; they were the ones to give Aaron the blood, but as high priests on this special occasion, he had to handle the blood. On ordinary occasions any priest could do it.

Identification again was made with the ram of the burnt offering, and the sacrifice was handled in the same way as was done in 8:18–21.

Once the priests had made atonement for their sins, and since at this point there was no call for a guilt offering, they proceeded to yield themselves to God in the dedication offering. They and the people were reminded of their human weaknesses, so, before the priests could minister for the people, there had to be a total commitment in a public dedication of the new religious leaders on the occasion of their installation.

People's offerings (vv. 15–21)

Having offered the sacrifices for himself and his sons, Aaron was ready to minister on behalf of the people. In order and in the prescribed manner 1) a male goat (the most expensive of the common people's offerings) was offered as a sin offering (literally, "he made *it* sin," a reminder of the exchange-of-life principle); 2) then a calf and a lamb were offered as a burnt sacrifice (representative of the herd and the flock); 3) finally, the memorial portion was presented for the meal offering (vv. 15–17).

An ox (special for this occasion) and a ram were next sacrificed as fellowship or peace offerings in the prescribed manner (vv. 18–21). There was one notable exception. The fat and breast were waved as a wave offering, and the fat was burned; but the right thigh was also treated as a wave offering instead of a heave offering as in 7:32. In the installation service all the priests could share in the joy of the occasion by partaking of the breast and of the right thigh of the animal.

In this ministry Aaron the high priest represented the people before God. Atonement was made to God, dedication was given, and thankfulness was expressed. The Lord was pleased to accept these heartfelt offerings, and on the day of the installation of Israel's priests the peoples' obedience to the revealed truths was confirmed by God. God thus instituted the schoolmaster that would teach Israel how to know the Lord and would ultimately point to the Messiah, who would in Himself fulfill all these things.

Benediction and intercession (vv. 22–23)

After Aaron had completed the prescribed offerings on behalf of the elect people of Israel, he blessed them as the Lord had prescribed (Num. 6:24–26). As he lifted up his hands, hands bloodied from the various offerings, he spoke words of mercy and peace (v. 22) and then entered into the tabernacle (v. 23). Perhaps we can see some similarity in the events of the ratification of the New Covenant, when Jesus Christ demonstrated dedication after He had made atonement for sin, and then lifted up his scarred hands and blessed His disciples (Luke 24:50). Having done so, He parted from them to enter His Father's house, from which He will return again someday (Luke 24:51).

As to the purpose Aaron and Moses had for entering the tent of meeting, one can only conjecture. Possibly Moses, as the representative of the Lord, committed into Aaron's keeping as well as into his sons' the vessels and order of the sanctuary. Perhaps there was also intercession before the Lord on behalf of themselves as well as on behalf of the people.

Glory (v. 24)

Coming out of the tent of meeting later, Moses and Aaron further blessed the people, and while they were doing so, the glory of the Lord appeared. This was the very presence of God in their midst, and some of that glory flashed on the altar to completely consume the sacrificial portions. With the installation of the priesthood the Shekinah of God put the final stamp of approval on what had been done in accordance with His instructions. When the people saw what had happened, they shouted and fell on their faces in worship.

In the same way God put His stamp of approval on the ministry of Jesus, particularly when it became dark as He hung on the cross during the last three hours of His suffering. As He died, the veil of the temple was torn in two from top to bottom. God also gave glory to the Son by raising Him from the dead on the third day. Someday He is to return, recognizable by the wounds He bears, to institute His kingdom. Would to God that many today would recognize the glory of God upon Jesus the Messiah, the Redeemer from sin, and the One who gives new life. May the recognition of this glory upon Jesus cause people to fall on their faces before Him and acknowledge Him.

C. Necessity of Careful Observance of God's Word (10:1–20)

Right after the installation Aaron and his sons began to minister on behalf of the people, and what should have been an auspicious and joyous beginning of a ministry of glory only too quickly turned into a ghastly experience. Because of this we should be always forewarned; when God has shown his glory and blessings, Satan is ever present to upset and tarnish His purposes. The lesson to remember always is that whenever God has done some great wonder for us, He leaves room for testing, either so that we may resist temptation and thereby develop morally or so that when we fail, we may learn sadly that there is wickedness in the depths of our hearts that causes us to mock God. So it was at the inception of the ministry of the Mosaic constitution.

The offense (v. 1)

Two of the sons of Aaron were not attentive to the proper way to worship God, and therefore were disobedient to His will. Nadab and Abihu were involved in the offer of "strange fire." We don't know exactly what this disobedience consisted of, but it has been suggested, probably incorrectly, that these two were drunk, a conjecture based on the injunction given in verse 9.

There is another possibility, however. The two sons had seen Aaron go into the tent of meeting to minister, and it could very well have been true that they became jealous of their father's position. *They* wanted to burn incense, and so they proceeded to take fire and the incense in order to go into the Holy Place, and even into the Holy of Holies. This seems to be the explanation, as given in 16:1–2. Nadab and Abihu deliberately disobeyed the word of God and asserted themselves in the process of handling sacred things!

Punishment (vv. 2–3)

The word "discipline" sounds like a strange word today. If everyone can live according to the dictates of his conscience in a social context in which standards are relative at best, then what is the point of discipline or punishment? The God of Israel was not and is not the God of the relative (situation ethics). He was not some mere tribal deity expressing His capricious displeasure. He is the God of the universe and has absolute standards, e.g., the Ten Commandments. He demands proper procedure by those who approach Him. Just because He does not punish or discipline those who break His standards everyday is no reason to think He will not have His reckoning at some time and in some place (1 Tim. 5:24–25)! Therefore, at the very inception of the sacrificial system, He had to punish sin severely.

Can one measure the effect on and the horror of the people when God killed Nadab and Abihu? The death of the sons could have occurred even while worshipers were coming with their sacrifices. The judgment on Nadab and Abihu was public in character and happened on a profoundly solemn occasion. God wanted the people to understand the meaning of His holy character. Through the law God showed Himself plenteous in mercy and grace but never at the expense of holiness. Is this Old Testament principle not to be found in the New Testament? We are reminded of the deaths of Ananias and of Sapphira (Acts 5) and of the untimely deaths referred to in 1 Corinthians 11:30. The holiness of God never changes. He is to be worshiped in accordance with His word and will, and He is always to be first in our affections. In the face of this truth and its visible consequences, Aaron bowed his head in humble silence.

Priestly purity (vv. 4–7)

Two elements entered the picture at this point, both indicating God's love and care for Aaron and his two remaining sons. First, God did not want Aaron and his other sons to take part in removing the bodies of their beloved for burial, thereby sparing them further emotional involvement. Two relatives of Aaron, who were Levites, took the bodies for burial outside the camp.

Second, Aaron and his remaining two sons were not dismissed from the priesthood but rather continued to function as Israel's representatives before God. But as priests in their office, they could not go forth on this occasion from the place of worship, nor could they show signs of mouring such as uncovering of the head and tearing of the clothes. For Aaron and his sons to mourn or to leave their public posts at this time would seem to question God's action. By Aaron's actions the people were given an example of how to accept the justice of God so that further judgment upon the congregation would be avoided. Jesus, our High Priest, while He did weep at times, would not be deterred from His duty. The congregation mourned, however, because God, through Moses, allowed them to.

Reiteration of duties and privileges (vv. 8–15)

New injunctions were given to safeguard the holy things. While the priests ministered in the service of the tabernacle, they were not to partake of any alcoholic beverages, no matter what the occasion. Contrary to the examples of Nadab and Abihu, the ministers of the Lord in the tabernacle were to be clear of head and heart in order to obey faithfully the word of the Lord. In this way they could be a good testimony and be able to teach the people God's word (v. 11). This is also the example for believer-priests today, particularly those in places of leadership.

Aaron and his surviving sons were reminded again of the high privilege of serving in their office. Moses reminded the priests that they were entitled to portions of foods from the various sacrifices. Even after what had happened to Nadab and Abihu, God reminded Aaron and his surviving sons that they would still have the high and holy privilege of receiving food from the peace offerings. As God cared for and loved them, so He loves us even in the midst of the most extreme pressures. We can still sit at God's table and realize that He is ever mindful of our needs.

Error and grace (vv. 16–20)

Moses searched diligently for the goat of a sin offering brought by some civil ruler (4:22) or some lay person (4:28) and discovered that it had been burned up in the fire. Upon learning this, Moses was angry and chided the two surviving sons of Aaron for their error. Not only was food for the priests lost, but the type teaching was also marred. It was serious indeed to mishandle this offering.

Aaron, Spirit-filled but heavy-hearted, answered Moses wisely with a wisdom that comes sometimes with grief and sorrow (v. 19). He reminded Moses that two of his sons had, in the beginning of the day, presented their sin and burnt offerings for themselves before setting out to minister on behalf of the Israelites. Now they were dead. Aaron and his two surviving sons remained alone in the tabernacle as representatives of the nation, and in their grief they had mishandled one goat sin offering. Aaron ruefully asked Moses whether God would really have been pleased if he and his remaining sons had eaten of the sin offering? In other words, Aaron was asking for mercy because of his grief-filled heart, even though he did not demonstrate his upset condition.

When Moses heard these words, although he was zealous for the word of God, he was moved too, since the two wayward sons were his nephews. Notice the similarity here between Moses and Christ. Moses was faithful in all his house, and he truly felt for his people (Heb. 3:2, 5); so Christ in the same way is touched with the feeling of our infirmities, and though He is holy and cannot countenance sin, He loves us and feels deeply for us in our sorrows and griefs (Heb. 4:15).

For Further Study

1. In a Bible dictionary or encyclopedia (see bibliography) read articles on: anoint, consecration, ephod, ordination, Urim and Thummim.

2. The breastplate stones and shoulder stones of Aaron had the names of the clans of Israel engraved on them. Show how this particular symbolism relates to the priesthood of believers today.

3. Why is the high priest singled out for his consecration for office, even more than the civil authority (even king in later history of Israel prior to Babylonian exile)?

4. Review and list the steps involved in the consecration and installation of the priests. Can any of these steps relate to service by believers today?

5. Why should God judge so severely the actions of Nadab and Abihu? Is this severity of judgment limited only to the Old Testament?

6. Can two opposites, error and grace, coexist?

Chapter 4

Laws of Purification
(Leviticus 11:1–15:33)

Up to this point the sacrificial system and the priests who administered this system have been the topics of concern. The emphasis has been on the approach to God through atonement, dedication, and thanksgiving on the part of the people as well as the priests. It was proper to begin on this note in order to show that God takes the initiative in reaching the hearts of men.

Now a different aspect will be underscored. Beginning with this chapter, God spelled out the way Israel was to be separated from that which was unclean through various models of worship and dimensions of life style. Laws were given to Israel to distinguish between the right and wrong ways to live, to learn God's feeling about sin, and to find out how to avoid it. When the people did sin by becoming unclean, they (or the priesthood) had the sacrificial and ritual counterparts of the law that were needed to instruct and lead the people into atonement and cleansing.

A. The Diet of God's People (11:1–47)

Strange as it may seem, holiness and separation included even what one put in his mouth. This was not merely for reasons of hygiene, although there was some emphasis on that. There was a more spiritual reason.

The dietary laws (vv. 1–23)

Of those animals Israelites were permitted to eat, the rule was quite specific: the animal had to be one which chewed the cud and also had its hoof divided so that it had split hooves (v. 3). An animal that chewed the cud was not carnivorous but lived rather on vegetable food, an important distinction.

Concerning the splitting of the hoof, it was important that there was a complete dividing of the hoof. By this rule were excluded such animals as the lion and the dog, whose feet have a membrane that unites the claws. These animals are usually carnivorous and were forbidden as food.

As to marine life only that which had *both* fins and scales could qualify for food. There was need for this law because there was hardly a tribe that was not near some body of water, e.g., the Mediterranean, the Sea of Galilee, the Waters of Merom, the Jordan River, and other tributary streams.

Concerning fowls every clean bird could be eaten; to facilitate selection of birds that were clean, the Scripture eliminates those birds considered unclean (see also Deut. 14:11–20). Lest there be any problem as to the criterion of selection, the fowls listed as unclean were carnivorous. Israelites could also include certain insects in their diets, even though this choice of food may seem questionable to Westerners. The only insects considered edible were winged insects that walked on all fours and had jointed legs above their feet, enabling them to hop (v. 21). Edible insects, then, were limited to the various kinds of devastating locusts, crickets or beetles, and the grasshoppers. All other insects were unclean, including all flies, bees, etc. Reptiles and worms were not permitted to be eaten either.

Further clarification of doubtful situations was given: certain animals may have chewed the cud, but their hooves were not fully split, or vice versa; e.g., the camel, though it chewed its cud, could not be eaten because its hooves were not completely divided, and the pig, while it has a cloven hoof, did not chew its cud.

The rule for marine life was to avoid anything that did not have both fins and scales. It was forbidden to eat fowl that gorged themselves on other creatures or fed on dead flesh or had unclean practices. Those insects that went on all four legs, or those with many feet, or those that went on their bellies were forbidden as food.

Defilement (vv. 24–40)

Death defiles because it is a reminder of the curse of the Fall, and while the Israelite could not prevent the occurrence of death, he was not to come near it unnecessarily, much less touch or pick up any carcass of an animal that died of itself. In touching or picking up any dead body, a person became unclean, and he had to wash his clothes; ritually, he remained unclean until evening, or from the Jewish point of view, until the next day (since the Jewish day began with sundown). The washing reminds one of the need for cleanliness and separation from the defiled thing. There was also a delayed restoration to the community for two reasons: 1) to prevent the spreading of anything contagious; and 2) to provide time for the person to reflect on the reasons that God's laws spelled out what was clean or unclean. (Instructions were also given concerning anyone who touched creeping things and the restoration to the community by cleansing [vv. 26–31]. There was no need for the washing of clothes in this case since this contact with defilement was a momentary, accidental one).

Sensitivity to contact with death as defilement was further emphasized: any article in a house touched by a dead body had to be soaked in water until evening, when it was considered clean again (vv. 32–40). If anything dead fell into an earthenware or clay pot, the pot had to be broken because there was no way for such a pot to be ceremonially cleansed (see 6:28). Food or liquids touched by any dead body became unclean. Ovens (usually made of earthenware) for baking food and what are possibly special kinds of cooking pots with lids had to be smashed if they were polluted. The last restriction might sound extremely harsh, but it must be remembered that cooking utensils soak up flavor and that they could have soaked up something from a dying, unclean creature, rendering the cooking implements unclean. Israelites, as an elect people, were to learn what genuine separation meant, experiencing in everyday life the difference between the holy and the profane. Careful instructions were also given for caring for proper hygiene when dead bodies fell into cisterns or onto seed for sowing. There is an interesting point of hygiene regarding wet seed; dampness would rapidly spread any contamination, and therefore this seed was thrown away.

Summary (vv. 41–47)

Moses summed up the message concerning the dietary rules. Holiness was not something to strive for only on a Sabbath day, but rather it was to be an everyday experience, even involving what was to be eaten. Though the details concerning cleanliness were meticulous, many times the attention paid to the very small details of life ensure genuine holiness. It was not God's wish to prompt a robotlike obedience in His call for separation. The Lord reminded Israel that He indeed had delivered His people from Egyptian bondage, based on His great love for them but that He was calling His people to be holy because holiness was the very essence of His nature. The nearer they drew to their God, the more they were to be separated from sinful secular and pagan practices and were to exhibit the character of God.

Purpose of the dietary rules

We now need to explore some reasons for the restrictions in the dietary rules. One of the points made in this discussion was that the meat that was considered clean came from creatures eating grass, grain, and herbs, while the meat of carnivorous creatures was forbidden. The main reason for these dietary rules was primarily theological and not hygienic. It has already been pointed out that life and blood are synonymous, and that to partake of blood, therefore, was considered a heinous practice. The blood of any creature stood for the life of that creature. So an Israelite did not eat any creature which ate bloody prey. There was to be a high regard for life and this figured in what was to be considered clean, and consequently it related to holiness.

For this reason dietary laws were developed concerning even the way clean animals were to be killed and eaten, or what would be considered kosher. The living creature to be eaten had its jugular vein cut, and the blood of the creature was carefully allowed to drain from the carcass. Before the meat was processed for food, as much of the blood as possible was removed. This practice is designed to respect life, symbolized by blood.

The second, and also important, purpose for distinguishing between clean and unclean flesh concerned the hygienic and sanitary element. Many forms of life do not prey on other forms, but because of the latter animals' eating and living habits, they are considered unfit for food, e.g., swine wallowing in the mud and eating things considered unclean can become disease carriers so that their flesh was considered unfit for human consumption. There was also the consideration of various forms of life liable to poisoning, e.g., lobsters, which if not killed properly become tainted.

A third reason for the necessity of dietary laws was the lack of refrigeration. It was a formidable enough task to distinguish what was fit for food and what wasn't, but there was also the problem of keeping it. Because the Middle East is mostly quite warm, it was impossible to keep meat preserved from one day to the next. Therefore, meat was rarely kept overnight, except in extraordinary circumstances, e.g., the vow offering (7:16). Even with all our modern refrigerating procedures, we cannot guarantee that meat will not spoil; meats can also be diseased, even before they are refrigerated.

Regardless of these purposes there was always the element of the holy. Theological and hygienic reasons guided the Israelite to glorify God and to do what was best for his own welfare.

New Testament application

Many Christians regard the dietary laws as being local and temporary for Israel alone, believing that the church today is universal, world-wide, and exists in all kinds of climates. Therefore, say they, Christians are not restricted as to what they can eat (see Acts 15:19). They defend not putting any restrictions on kinds of food by referring to Peter's vision, in which he was told to eat what he would not have eaten previously (Acts 10:12–16). While this writer recognizes the prerogatives of the church of God, yet there certainly are theological and hygienic reasons for making distinctions among foods.

(1) One needs to pay careful attention to the Jerusalem Council's decision (Acts 15:19, 20). It was the Jewish believer's feeling that Gentile believers were not to be burdened with the dietary rules except that Gentile believers were to kill their meat in a humane way and to make sure that all the blood was drained from the flesh. The theological reason for these two restrictions was so that the Gentile converts would recognize the sacredness of life as evidenced by the blood of the creatures to be eaten.

(2) However, no such instructions were given to Jewish believers. While it was recognized that the Jewish believer in Jesus as Messiah was no longer under the Mosaic constitution, there was still the ethnic factor to consider. Jewish believers, while free to eat all foods, could not have a taste for foods on which they had not been reared. Jewish believers also could keep the dietary rules as a means by which they could demonstrate their *ethnic* identity with their brethren, even as Paul did (1 Cor. 9:20), so as to share their faith in Jesus as Messiah and Redeemer with their Jewish brethren.

(3) A third reason for avoiding foods lawful to eat was the principle of abstinence so as not to offend. In doubtful cases as to what to eat,

especially as it concerns our witness, it is far better to lean to the side of abstinence than to run the risk of doing evil (1 Cor. 8:13).

(4) It was also needful to use some common sense in the choice of foods. If we know certain foods are not clean from a hygienic point of view or if it is suspected that some foods are disease carriers, it is best to avoid these foods. It is positively dangerous to eat certain marine life if they are not prepared in a very careful manner; so why run the risk of being needlessly sick if there might be a problem with a certain food?

B. Laws of motherhood (12:1–8)

Mothers were special objects of attention. A mother who had just given birth required purification because she had brought a sinner into the world (Job 25:4; Ps. 51:5).

If the child was a boy, the mother remained unclean for seven days outside the camp, or away from the general course of life, in accordance with the laws of a woman's monthly period. Blood had been shed in the childbirth, and the time for cleansing was seven days.

On the eighth day the newborn boy was circumcised (v. 3). Perhaps the reason for waiting until this day was to give time for those concerned to check the child's health. If the baby lived to the beginning of the second week, he was sufficiently strong for the ritual of circumcision. Perhaps another reason was that the child could be considered unclean from the mother's blood, and he too had to wait seven days to be considered ritually clean before circumcision admitted him into the fellowship of the Mosaic covenant.

After the cleansing of the seven days for the male, the mother could regain her family but continued in her purification (v. 4) for another thirty-three days. In the latter period she remained in partial seclusion and could not touch any consecrated thing nor enter the sanctuary area. The time for purification was a constant reminder that she had had a part in the transmission of sin in the human race. This was not to be regarded as anything degrading to the mother or her child, but rather there was the recurring theme of sin and the necessity for cleansing and salvation before her.

In the birth of a female the mother was unclean for twice as long as she was for a male child, fourteen days in uncleanness and sixty-six days in purification. It is difficult to assign a reason for this. Perhaps we might see a lesson in that when a mother gave birth to a female, other children would be born in the future; two females were involved in the birth, and therefore the periods for cleansing and for purification were doubled. There was then a double reminder of the transmission of sin.

In either birth the law of motherhood reminds us that we are sinners by nature and by birth. Every mother in Israel, then, after her days of purification, brought a one-year-old lamb for a burnt offering. She brought a pigeon or a dove for a sin offering to show her tie to the sinful human race, while the burnt offering was an expression of her dedication, particularly in her role of training up her child in the training and instruction of the Lord. In cases of poverty the mother could bring two doves or two pigeons, one for the sin offering and the other for the burnt offering.

One notes the extreme poverty of the family of Jesus when His mother, after her days of purification, brought either two doves or two pigeons (Luke 2:22–24) for her offerings. This also raises an interesting point inasmuch as Jesus' mother was obedient to the Law. She recognized by her offerings she was not free from sin as she went through the seven-day cleansing period, the thirty-three days of purification, and then presented a pigeon or a dove for her atonement from sin. And Jesus, born of such poor parents, certainly knew how to identify with those who sit in the very dust of the earth. The poor can enjoy the best that God has to offer because the blessed Son of God can speak their language.

C. Sanctification and Holiness (13:1–14:57)

Recognition of different diseases (13:1–46)

The laws of purification were further extended to control any outbreak of disease that could contaminate the Israelites. Laws were instituted to check and quarantine persons having even the possibility of any contagious disease that could affect even their approach to God. An elect people was taught that purity and holiness were separate and apart from disease. (See also Lev. 26:16b.)

The core of the lesson here was to demonstrate the relation between bodily disease and spiritual sin. Whenever an individual had a serious illness, it was not a sign that he was a terrible sinner; there are too many examples in the Old Testament of righteous people who were ill, some of whom were subsequently healed. But there is a basic truth to be learned under the Mosaic constitution—an emphasis that shows it was sin in the first place that introduced into the human race all the diseases to which man is subject. One of the judgmental aspects of sin is disease. The Israelite needed to know that the diseases he suffered were, generally speaking, brought about because of our first parents' disobedience and are the result of the curse (Gen. 3:17, 18). Therefore, these illnesses were not to be brought into the presence of God.

It should also be mentioned that the word rendered "leprosy" in the English versions for the Hebrew *sara'at*, with the corresponding description of symptoms in chapters 13 and 14, is not, medically speaking, the modern leprosy, called Hansen's disease. There is not space to cite the many leprologists who have stated emphatically that the descriptions of leprosy in Leviticus 13 are not those of leprosy as it is known today.

Leviticus 13:6 definitely speaks of an infection that was not permanent but was only a local skin eruption that began to heal after only seven days. There is also reference to a deep-seated ulcer (13:7) that was more than a mild break in the skin and that may have been of the nature of a phagedemic ulcer that would spread and not heal. Scales are also mentioned (13:30), which is a scabby disease of the skin, especially of the scalp, possibly synonymous with psoriasis. There are two details in the Levitical record that cannot apply to leprosy today—the whiteness described and the presence of the disease on the scalp. Doctors have stated that leprosy lesions are never white, that leprosy of the scalp is extremely rare, and that it occurs only in very advanced lepromatous leprosy and never as a first symptom. Each of the Levitical descriptions of leprosy relate to one of the various skin diseases, but not to classical or modern leprosy. This is not to suggest that leprosy did not exist; it is only that the symptoms indicated in Leviticus 13 do not describe the dreaded leprosy of which we have heard so often.

Sara'at literally means "a mark, a stroke," and can refer to a host of skin disorders. Some of these were extremely serious and required immediate separation from the people of Israel and the sanctuary until there was a healing. However, most of the diseases indicated here were among the numerous skin problems with which the human flesh can be afflicted, although these were not to be treated lightly. Furthermore, once it is understood that *sara'at* is not one disease but any one of several afflictions, then the problem of plagues in vessels, garments, and houses is solved. The description of growths, fungi, and infections in these articles and places is not characteristic of genuine leprosy but can easily describe various skin diseases and fungi.

Leviticus 13 specifies various skin diseases: infections (v. 2), deep-seated ulcers (vv. 7–8), swelling (v. 10), boils (v. 19), infections as the result of a burn (v. 24), scales or scabs (v. 30), white spots of eczema (vv. 38–39), and infections on the bald head or forehead (v. 42).

While the physical examination of the diseases seems to have been tedious and complicated, certain symptoms appeared to be the key factors for which the priests looked. Was the skin lower than the surrounding skin at the point of the infection? Was the flesh open and raw, or was the skin area in question reddish white (as in the case of any infection on the bald forehead in v. 42)? Did the hair turn yellowish or white at an infected area because of fever, etc.? At the time of the giving of the law, while there were no doubt medical practitioners to detect these diseases, and while some priests could have been trained physicians, yet enough medical information was given to all the priests so that they would be the ones to formally pronounce one either sick or well or to determine whether a person should be quarantined to check the progress of the infection or disease.

It was the theocratic representative of God, the priest, and not some secular or civil functionary, who made the medical pronouncement as to whether one was sick or well. Furthermore, having leprosy or not having it was not a case of merely being sick or well. The designation of being clean or unclean was also important; for again the theological angle of the origin of human illness, i.e., sin, appeared. This process of purification strongly emphasized the Israelite's relationship to God under the covenant. The people were not to be silent observers with no responsibility, but when a priest called someone unclean, responsibility and holiness were vividly underscored (vv. 45–46).

The one declared unclean was sent outside the camp, and his clothes were torn as a sign of mourning and woe. He was separated from the elect people, illustrating the state of a sinner under sentence of death. The hair was disheveled, which was also illustrative of mourning. His upper lip was covered, indicating that he could not come near to men to speak but that all he could say was, in warning, "Unclean! Unclean!" to avoid passing his disease on to someone else. He was in physical separation and in anguish, cut off from family, friends, and all the people. At such a time the lessons of the nature of sin as well as its consequences of spiritual separation became apparent to him and to anyone else who was ill.

But God is not inhumane! Rather, He is eager that we learn to partake of His gracious provision. Fortunately, most of these skin diseases or illnesses ran their course, and ultimately there was healing. It was to be hoped that the sick (and also unclean person), because of this severe lesson of separation, would turn to God and cry out for spiritual redemption and healing in much the same way many people today come to the Lord. Many are the saints who can testify that it was on the sick bed in a hospital room, shut away from the outside world, that they cried out for salvation as well as for healing. The ancient Israelite was no different, and often he could testify that it was his illness that had brought him closer to the Lord.

It is not implied that every sick person in the Old Testament suffered because of evil doing. But whatever the case, the agony of separation afflicted both unclean and clean and moved the Israelite to turn to God for forgiveness. In the same way Jesus, our High Priest, stands ready to give us a new life, to make us clean, and to bring us from our separation to the full fellowship of the family of God.

Disease and fungus in clothing (13:47–59)

The laws of purification also related to all the material possessions owned by the people of God. Sometimes diseases, infections, rot, etc., do not originate in the person but in the world around us. It also has been cursed and is therefore subject to attack by harmful attacks of bacteria.

The Israelite was to carefully watch his clothing: wool (from the animal world), linen (from the plant world), leather (some skin product), etc. It didn't matter whether the clothes were inexpensive or expensive; if any clothing showed signs of fungus, rot, etc., it was to be brought to the priests for examination. Ample opportunity was given to save the clothing through time and washings, but if the garment remained infested, it had to be consigned to the fire.

The Israelite was to learn that even though his clothes were clean, other people had to be protected from anything contagious. And, the health aspect was not the only aspect considered. There was also the matter of theological cleanness and uncleanness that related to the curse on creation. The purification rules were reminders to people that they were to be clothed with garments of the righteousness of God through salvation and with the garments of dedication through consecration.

There is certainly a New Testament moral and spiritual application at this point. Jude warns that our garments are to be kept clean (v. 23). Because of the Mosaic injunction one did not dare wear contaminated clothing for fear of contracting a skin disorder. The Jude passage (and others such as Rev. 3:4) suggests a deeper meaning; the garment can be a symbol of whatever there is about ourselves that, through the various ways in which we have opportunity of contact with the world around us, contributes to the moral destruction of wicked men. And as believers we are warned that our clothes (that is, our every contact) can be spotted and marked by the world around us. A call also goes out to unbelievers to exchange their unclean garments for what Jesus Christ wants to provide for them; actually, Jesus wants to effect a change in the unbeliever so that there can be a moral and spiritual revitalization. We today can do no less than the Israelites; we too are called to a holiness of person and a holiness concerning our relationship with the world.

Pronouncement of healing (14:1–32)

Just as the Law was strict in separating those with disease, so the Law was equally as gracious in restoring one healed of his illness. It must be observed that no man, in an ultimate sense, could ever effect the healing. No doubt the person with a disease could have sought means for a cure, but at the same time he had to call on the Lord, who provides recovery in the last analysis. This truth became apparent when the priest went to examine one who had been healed. While permission was given for the separated one to proceed with the ritual of cleansing, all would realize that the priest could only pronounce one clean; he could not heal. Only God could do that. Today, unlike the Levitical priest, Jesus as our High Priest restores us, enables us to be spiritually healed in redemption, and in many situations (although not in every case) He also provides physical healing.

The first step (vv. 1–9)

The procedure of cleansing was quite complicated, but it is rich in its detail of precious truths. The officiating priest gave orders, probably to relatives of the recovered person, that they bring two live, ritually clean birds, cedar wood, a scarlet string, and hyssop. The priest then instructed that one of the birds be killed so that its blood could be caught in an earthenware (clay) pot which already contained running, i.e., fresh water. The use of an earthenware vessel stressed the uniqueness of this situation, for after the vessel was used once, it was never to be used again. The blood in this vessel was used in the restoration of *this one particular person*, and afterwards the vessel was to be destroyed (see Lev. 6:28).

With the death of the bird (since it became identified with the Israelite's physical illness) we are reminded of the lesson of the exchange-of-life principle. To be restored to the community, once having been removed from it, the Israelite also had the requisite of having a new physical life. Both the recovered persons as well as other healthy Israelites had to realize this most important lesson. The life of the bird that was killed was symbolically given to the recovered Israelite. But obviously there was a deeper lesson for all concerned in the restoration of the formerly ill person. The restored person was reminded of the necessity of a new spiritual life and of his need to truly know God.

The running or fresh water (vv. 5–6) was symbolic of cleansing and purification. Running water was a picture of the carrying away of the uncleanness of the flesh, so that the restored Israelite was cleansed from his sickness. In the New Testament counterpart there are many aspects of purification and cleansing, either by the blood of Christ or by the action of the Word (John 15:3), that show these aspects of restoration and purification in Leviticus to be very important.

The priest took the live bird, and the cedar wood and hyssop which was tied together by the scarlet string, and dipped them all into the earthen pot which contained the running (fresh) water and the blood (the symbol of a new life) of the slain bird (v. 6). See also verse 51. With both the blood and the water on the bird, with the cedar wood, and with the hyssop the priest sprinkled the restored person seven times, pronouncing him clean, and then freed the bird so it could fly away. Each of these objects and actions is meaningful.

Cedar wood has the property of deterring decay and corruption. The hyssop, with its pungent fragrance, also opposes decay and corruption. The scarlet string, tying the cedar wood and hyssop together, represented the blood that would cleanse from sin. The thread holding the cedar wood and hyssop together was an indication that these objects were needed in this special instance concerning what was required for full restoration. Using the water with the blood emphasized that the restored person was being cleansed by receiving a new physical life, while the sevenfold sprinkling was a perfect action. The total symbolism highlighted the picture of purifying the restored Israelite.

The live bird, sprinkled with blood and associated symbolically with the physical illness, was set free over the open field so that the restored person in a dramatic way learned that his old life had vanished and that he would never face this particular corruption again. This concept will be seen again in the Day of Atonement procedure in Leviticus 16, but a precious truth is emphasized here. In cleansing, the Lord provides atonement for the old sin nature of the restored person so that he can be completely assured of his forgiveness, provided he will appropriate for himself the all-important lesson of atonement in the ritual of cleansing and restoration. As we already indicated, the purposes of this ritual were not only to point up the need for physical purification but also to demonstrate clearly the lesson of spiritual salvation. In the type fulfillment Jesus assures us that He will take away our sins so that we never have to be confronted by them again!

Finally, the healed person washed his clothes, shaved off all his hair, and then bathed (v. 8). Washing was a part of the purification procedure, while the shaving of the hair was a further precaution to ascertain full healing. The Israelite was then permitted into the camp, but he could not yet join his family for seven days. Then, if the healing was confirmed, the restored one shaved every hair off his body and washed himself and his clothes. He was then ready for the final procedure in the restoration process.

The second step (vv. 10–32)

The restored Israelite was not as yet fully admitted into the fellowship of ministry and service among the people. There were further steps to be taken for a full dedication and anointing before the Israelite was permitted to function once more within the elect nation. Seven days had gone by after he had been admitted into the camp, and during this period a close watch was kept on him so that final approval as to healing could be given.

Finally, on the eighth day the restored person brought the appropriate offerings, recognizing the past from which he had been delivered as well as the future and asking for dedication and anointing. Both the officiating priest and the Israelite appeared before the door of the tent of meeting, as if before the Lord Himself. The priest took one of the male lambs as well as a pint of oil and waved them before the Lord. It is interesting to note that the first offering, the male lamb, was presented as a trespass offering, contrary to the procedure already described in chapters 4 and 5. Perhaps the emphasis here was on the particular sin of which the Israelite was aware, yet it was a reminder that one of the effects of sin from the original Fall was illness.

Besides handling the slaughter of the lamb and the blood of the guilt offering, the priest performed another feature that emphasized the forgiveness of the particular sin of which this Israelite had been guilty. The priest took some of the blood of the guilt offering and put it on the lobe of the Israelite's right ear, on his right thumb, and on the big toe of his right foot (v. 14), a procedure similar to that in the consecration of the priests. This symbolism of the restoration also had a spiritual emphasis in showing the redemption of the person's spiritual hearing, obedience, service, and walk. Obviously, the reference to these parts of the body referred to the very person involved in the purification process. In the same way our restoration by Jesus today accomplishes forgiveness for sin's impairment.

Seven times the priest sprinkled oil before the Lord at the doorway of the tent (later, in the specified area at the front of the temple). This oil, symbol of the Holy Spirit, signified that this Israelite was being restored to the fellowship of the congregation and therefore was also a call for the Holy Spirit of God to come upon this one who had been separated from the fellowship. As if in answer, the officiating priest put some of the oil (again, as in the ritual with blood) upon the Israelite's right ear lobe, thumb, and big toe. This smearing of oil was the sign that the Israelite's hearing, obedience, service, and walk were being anointed by the Holy Spirit afresh for full participation in the community's worship and service. Similarly, after receiving the salvation offered us in Jesus Christ for the forgiveness of our sins, the Holy Spirit takes up His residence in our hearts so as to seal us into the family of God (Eph. 1:13–14). He not only seals us, however; He also anoints us for service, an anointing by which we can truly please Him.

Then, as if to emphasize full forgiveness, the officiating priest anointed the head of the restored Israelite with the remainder of the oil, an assuring sign and seal of his forgiveness and restoration and anointing. It was then possible for him to enter into full participation with the elect community. Certainly everyone in the congregation of Israel, as well as the family and friends involved with the recovered one, would hopefully learn firsthand what forgiveness meant, and there would be a call for them through this experience to seek spiritual redemption.

The rest of the offerings completed the formalities. A female lamb was killed and offered in the prescribed manner as the sin offering, and the remaining male lamb was presented as a burnt offering. Along with the lamb there was also the offer of the usual flour and grain offering mixed with oil for the dedication of this one's forthcoming work. After this complete ritual the Israelite had his full rights in the congregation restored as a personal testimony of what the living God had done. How our hearts rejoice and are filled with praise today that the Lord did not turn away from the awful sight of sinful men; rather, He took pity and sent His Son, the Messiah and Savior, to deliver us from our wretched condition so that we can be "to the praise of his glorious grace, which He has freely given us in the One he loves" (Eph. 1:6).

God always has been gracious with His people and in a situation during which an Israelite had suffered from a disease, it could well have been that the family also suffered great economic reverses, especially if the afflicted one was the breadwinner. Therefore, when the time arrived for the restoration of an Israelite, and if the family at that time was not able to afford the expensive sacrifices already mentioned, God provided in the Law for more modest offerings (v. 21ff.). The male lamb remained the same for the trespass offering, along with the same amount of oil, but two turtledoves or two pigeons were permitted for the sin and the burnt offerings. In addition, 1/10th of an ephah of flour for the grain offering was acceptable instead of the 3/10ths normally specified. What is important is that the family was not excused from bringing offerings. The restored Israelite had to realize that not only is sin costly but that there was also the type to be demonstrated.

Restoration of the sinner cost God His own Son, the Messiah. We must never think, even as the recovered Israelite learned, that the forgiveness of sin is cheap or that there is no price involved. Shame on us if we think that grace is cheap when salvation is offered freely to all sinners. It cost God dearly. At the same time it also calls for the complete dedication of our redeemed lives for God's service. We are not our own, for we are bought with a price so as to glorify God with our bodies (1 Cor. 6:20)!

Fungi and diseases in the house (14:33–53)

As bodies and even garments are subject to disease and fungi because of the curse on creation as a result of our first parents' disobedience, so the Israelite was taught (and we are too) that the earth itself was placed under a curse and that it has affected the very houses where people live. Houses can be subject to fungus, rot, mildew, etc., reminding us how far-reaching the curse was (and is).

When anyone staked all he had on things of this life, his materialism could become a mockery if contamination struck. The Israelite who encountered fungus or disease in his home was to connect the calamity with his needed dependence on the Lord. The curse God placed upon the earth was a constant reminder of an imperfect world with imperfect people in it. Contact with the world with its curse and its consequences was to serve as an incentive to Israelites to seek the salvation and spiritual redemption portrayed in the sacrificial system. We are likewise reminded in many ways of the fact that our possessions can be corrupted in the imperfect world in which we live and of the necessity to flee to Christ, the everlasting Rock. He is the only One who can give us life eternal, a life which never can be corrupted.

Moses next gave instructions concerning the action to be taken for contaminated houses. Every step possible was taken to save the house: quarantine, removal of affected stones and replacement with new ones, the scraping of all plaster on the walls and replastering. If the contamination persisted, the house was destroyed.

After the replacement of new blocks or stones in the original house, if it was then found to be free from contamination, the priest pronounced the house clean. At this juncture the owner had to provide for its ceremonial cleansing in the same way a healed Israelite was restored, as was discussed earlier. A holy people had to be separated to their God; therefore, there could be no contamination in their midst. Physical contamination only pointed up the spiritual need and the necessity to be free from the contamination of the soul.

The law also carefully stated that no one was to go into contaminated houses while they were sealed and were awaiting the priest's pronouncement. If the Israelite went into the house even for any of his things, he was regarded as unclean until the evening. If anyone went into such a house to eat or to lie down to sleep, he was unclean until evening, and he also had to wash his clothes. The word of God impressed standards of cleanliness upon the Lord's people so that they could come into line more and more with His standards and ultimately acquire a sensitivity to His holiness. It is also a lesson to us that we, under grace, have no reason to take lightly the holiness of God.

Conclusion (14:54–57)

This specific piece of legislation came to an end here. Diseases of the flesh, infected garments, diseased houses—all were intended to make the Israelite aware that he moved in a world of sin, that he was always in the midst of evil. Yet at the same time, there was always a way to escape, a way to find relief, physical as well as spiritual. Every opportunity was given for the Israelite to find salvation and to live blessedly, serving the Lord. We have this same opportunity today, no matter who we are or where we are. Jesus challenges us, "Behold, I am coming soon! My reward is with me, and I will give to everyone according to what he has done" (Rev. 22:12). We are also encouraged by Jesus: "My prayer is not that you take them out of the world, but that you protect them from the evil one" (John 17:15).

Unique legislation for body cleanliness (15)

Instructions were given to Moses and Aaron concerning some diseases of a body discharge as well as information on the ways people were to deal with some of the normal male and female functions. This type of legislation was unique among contemporary codes in the Middle East. God, in this legislation, regulated these functions so that they were put on a high moral plane because He insisted upon respect for the individual. Physical impunity connected with these functions meant uncleanness in a hygienic sense, yet again the paramount theological meaning behind the right use of these functions related to holiness.

When a man had a discharge from his body, he was regarded as unclean. This situation was not considered as serious as the diseases described in chapter 13, but this condition also had its dangers. What was exactly involved here we are not told except in general terms, but the judgment of being unclean was pronounced upon the disease.

Whatever or whomever the unclean person touched also became unclean. Not only did this legislation mark what was unclean, but isolation was enforced upon what or whom was declared as unclean. One can imagine what this would involve in a daily round of activities when an unclean person was quarantined to prevent any outbreak of possible disease. The usual rules for cleansing were applicable should anyone or anything become unclean, e.g., washing and then waiting until the evening to be considered clean again.

And again, this condition marked a definite tie between illness and sin, and as stated previously, the ill person may not have been involved in any direct wrong-doing himself; yet whenever there was an outbreak of sickness, the person's attention was focused on the relation of sin and illness. Besides heeding the precautions to avoid the spread of disease, Israel as an elect people also had to carefully consider their own spiritual relationship to God. Experiencing sickness and being healed constituted one more incentive to turn to the Lord and to stop any spread of spiritual apostasy and rebellion against God.

With the cessation of the discharge the man was to count off seven days, the standard check as to whether the illness was really over; if it was, he washed his clothes and bathed. On the eighth day he brought two turtledoves or two pigeons to the priest before the Lord at the tent door (or later, the temple), and the officiating priest offered them, one for a sin offering and the other for a burnt offering. The release from physical disability was to impress on the recovered man that not only was there a gracious release from illness, but there was also a spiritual redemption if he would avail himself of it. Not only would the man be impressed this way, but so would his family and friends. His experience would also be a testimony to all people involved so that they too could be challenged to consider their walk and relationship with the Lord. Sicknesses often remind us of the transitoriness of life and provide the incentive for us to turn to the Lord.

Instructions were also given concerning seminal emmision (vv. 16ff.). When this occurred, a man was to wash his body in water and separate himself until evening. Anything that came into contact with this emission was to be washed and not used until evening. When there were relations between a man and his wife, they were both to bathe and to wait until evening for cleansing. Note, however, that even though the affected persons or things were called unclean until evening, there was nothing after washing to imply any danger of disease. Rather, the Law's intention was to inculcate a respect for the potential of life in the emission. "Uncleanness" in this situation was really a positive emphasis on separation for proper control of this function.

The same could be said for the normal female function of a woman's period except that there is a greater complication for the woman than for the man because of the presence of blood. Here again the Law specified that everyone or everything she touched be considered unclean, requiring proper washing. If a husband had relations with his wife while she had her period, he would then be unclean along with his wife. For seven days whomever and whatever he touched would be unclean. If, seven days after the onset of the woman's period, the flow of blood stopped, she could bathe on the eighth day and resume her part in normal society. It must be emphasized that no negative concept was implied as being present in the matter of "uncleanness" on the part of a woman during her period (except if the law were disobeyed). Rather, there was the attempt again to inculcate proper respect for the potential life in the ovum.

Of course, if a woman had an illness causing a dysfunction not connected with her period, she had to remain separate as long as the flowing of blood was present. This was the case of the woman who had had a hemorrhage for twelve years and who came to Jesus to be healed (Luke 8:43ff.). One can well imagine her plight when for twelve years she had had to be separate from society's functions. We can also enter into her joy when without shame she testified of the healing of her dysfunction. As in a normal cleansing, a woman with such a malady had to wait a seven-day period to see whether the healing was accomplished, after which she was to go to the priest on the eighth day with two turtledoves or two pigeons. She was then to offer the birds, one for a sin offering and the other for a burnt offering. Once again, the relation between illness and sin was meant to be apparent. Perhaps no specific sin was assigned to a woman's dysfunction, but an emphasis on the effects of the Fall reminded her that the very nature of man is sinful. The offer of the bird for the sin offering was meant to impress upon the woman the need for the salvation of her soul while she was in the process of being restored to the community. Hopefully, this procedure would not be a mere ritual. God provided every possible opportunity for people to accept His prescribed approach for salvation.

Leviticus 15 closes with the warning that these instructions were to be faithfully kept because of the lessons inherent in these laws. To disobey them would be considered an affront to God Himself and to His presence as He dwelt among His people. God wanted a holy people to consider carefully the lessons of this chapter, which contributed to holiness, including the matter of being clean as well as having a proper respect for life. To have refused to have acknowledged these instructions could have brought death upon the disobedient one. We should not consider God's ways for the Israelites harsh, for there is also a call to holy living for us today, no less so now than for the people under the Mosaic constitution. Yes, the call should even be more urgently heeded today than at that time because we have a greater revelation of God in His Word than the Israelites did.

For Further Study

1. In a Bible dictionary or encyclopedia (see bibliography) read articles on: defile, disease(s), food, leprosy, uncleanness).

2. Review again the basic reason for linking holiness and foods permitted to be eaten. Why was blood so important?

3. If you invited both Jewish and Muslim persons to a restaurant, would you order and eat either roast pork or baked ham? Why or why not?

4. Discuss the special instructions governing the purification of a mother after she has given birth in connection with the transmission of the sin nature.

5. Make a study of the leprosy of the Bible and the disease known as leprosy that we know about today.

6. Who was responsible for healing the recovered leper? What was particularly unique about the Samaritan who turned to thank Jesus (Luke 17:11-19)?

Chapter 5

The Day of Atonement
and the Importance of Blood Atonement
(Leviticus 16:1–17:16)

We come now to the very heart of the sacrificial aspect of the Mosaic constitution. The Israelites were instructed as to the proper approach to God in the worship of the Day of Atonement. As if to emphasize its importance the names of the two rebellious sons of Aaron are not designated here, indeed an ominous note (10:1–2). The Word of God explicitly sets forth the necessity of meeting with Him and the *way* in which to do it. Aaron learned in a most painful way that it was fatal to flout God's law, which spelled out the correct way to come into His presence.

A. Purpose

There seems to have been a threefold purpose for the legislation that governed the observance of the Day of Atonement. First, although the presence of God dwelt in the sanctuary (later, the temple), the priests were not perfect. Every year the priests were reminded that they needed to be cleansed, as did every object in the sanctuary.

A second purpose was to remind the nation that her standing before the Lord was a concern for renewal year after year. Each one in the nation had to search his own soul concerning his relationship with the sovereign God, seeking to remove any barrier. The high priest also identified himself with the people in this national soul-searching, as he had to represent the nation. Had Israel genuinely continued to search their hearts throughout their long history, they would have been spared much grief.

A third purpose involved a call for *individuals* to repent and to seek the face of God. The Day of Atonement offering emphasized and made real the forgiveness and restoration of individuals who had offered sacrifices during the past year. But what of the individual who had failed to make a single offering for a whole year? He may have been stubborn when confronted by some particular sin and may have refused to do anything about it, or he could have had a tender heart but was entirely in the dark about some particular sin. Whatever the case, on the Day of Atonement everyone sought forgiveness for all sin, intentional or unintentional. Just as the nation as a whole could not go on from year to year without facing the need to repent and to seek forgiveness, even so individuals within the nation could not go from year to year without seeking forgiveness for sin.

In the Day of Atonement ritual were the means to impress upon the people the spiritual redemption God wanted for them. In the merciful provision of His Law God never intended that the nation should go through the ritual of the Day of Atonement as a mere formality, but hoped that people would find in the experience the salvation of their souls. In the meanwile, however, year by year the nation and the individuals in it were made positionally clean and pure because of God's patience. Today, while no Gentile nation has the same relationship to God as Israel had, God patiently presents the truths of the gospel in Jesus Christ again and again so that people can respond and receive the Savior.

B. The Sin Offering and Atonement

Aaron was instructed in the specific manner in which he and other high priests to follow were to enter the Holy of Holies inside the veil. No one except the high priest could stand before the mercy seat, which was on the ark; if anyone attempted to do so, he would die. Only once a year did the high priest enter the very presence of God, symbolized by the cloud over the mercy seat, with a precise procedure to follow. The holiness of God was therefore impressed on the people and the priests. Because of God's mercy He enabled the high priest, a mere man, to approach His presence to minister for himself and for the nation. What a lesson for people today! In the same way today there is only one way to approach God, i.e., through Jesus Christ as our High Priest. No man-made religion is sufficient to provide for forgiveness of sin.

Priest's ministry for himself

In ministering for himself, the high priest before dressing, first bathed as an act of cleansing (see ch. 8). Before he could minister for the people of Israel, he first had to be accepted as ceremonially worthy. Aaron and the high priests who followed him were made aware of their own shortcomings and had to seek forgiveness for their own sins first. In a special way the great Day of Atonement ritual for the high priest reminded him and the whole corps of priests that *they* were in need of salvation in the "exchange-of-life" principle.

After bathing, the high priest donned his garments: the linen undergarments, the linen tunic, the linen sash, and the linen turban. No ephod or breastplate was worn on this occasion because the high priest appeared simply as the head of the people in a humble manner, ministering for himself. Aaron then brought a bull for a sin offering for himself and his household (4:3). Two goats were also to be used in the ritual, and in selecting them lots were cast upon the goats to determine which would be killed as the sin offering for the people and which would be the scapegoat.

The high priest was then ready to offer the sacrifice on behalf of himself and his household. He killed the bull for the sin offering, and then, taking some of the blood of the bull, a fire pan full of coals from the altar of burnt offering, and two handfuls of finely ground sweet incense, he went into the Holy of Holies inside the veil or curtain (v. 12). There he put the incense on the fire before the Lord so that the ensuing cloud of incense covered the mercy seat and the whole area of the Holy of Holies. This had to be done so that the high priest would not die, as incense was always a symbol and picture of communion in prayer. The incense was specially prepared for this purpose (Exod. 30:34–37). and was used when the priests ministered at the altar of incense. Every New Testament reference to it connects incense and the use of it with prayer (Rev. 5:8; 8:3, 4). In humility and prayer the high priest sought acceptance by God.

But there also had to be the presentation of the blood of the bull, representing by identification a new life for the priest (v. 14). No high priest could ever come into the Holy of Holies without blood, as the symbol of new life provided by the bull for the high priest as well as for everyone of his household; the blood was a reminder that atonement was required for the imperfection of the person and the ministry of priests. The priest took some of the blood in his finger and sprinkled the mercy seat. This was seen as atonement for his offense against the person of God and as a sign that he needed a new life so as to stand righteous before God. Then he also sprinkled some of the blood with his finger seven times in front of the mercy seat as an acknowledgment of his need for atonement for his ministry before the Lord; the blood represented forgiveness and the gift of a new life, which God alone was able to provide. In a very graphic way the high priest recognized that both in his person and in his work ministry there was a personal need. God was gracious, however, and because of the sacrifice the high priest could enter the new year cleansed from his iniquities. Hopefully, the high priest would avail himself of the real meaning of the exchange-of-life principle and would truly know the Lord.

By contrast, the Mediator of the New Covenant, in His ministry, did not have to confess His sin because there was no sin in Him. Jesus the Messiah, acting in the capacity of High Priest, was holy, innocent, undefiled; He did not have to offer sacrifices for Himself before He could minister for us, taking our place perfectly before the exalted and holy God. Jesus alone faultlessly bridges the infinite gap between God and man, and because of His death, He can give us His life.

Priest's ministry for congregation

Having ministered on behalf of himself within the veil, or curtain, the high priest then served on behalf of the congregation of Israel. He took one of the goats for the sin offering, slaughtered it, and took some of its blood within the area of the veil to do as he had done with the blood of the bull, this time providing atonement for the sins of the sons of Israel against the person of God Himself and atonement for the imperfect ministry of the community. Israel was an elect nation, and she was God's servant, but obviously her service was an extremely imperfect one at best. The unbelievers in the community definitely needed an atonement. Even those who were godly in the congregation recognized their shortcomings. The application of the blood of the goat represented the collective life of the nation, judged because of sin. Through atonement the nation received, at least positionally, a new lease on life for the new year.

Atonement for tabernacle

There was also a need to cleanse the Holy Place because of the people's impurities (v. 16). The high priest took blood and sprinkled the area of the Holy Place, as well as the furniture: the table of show-bread, the lamp stand, and the altar of incense standing in front of the veil. In a sense the people were close to the presence of God, and this familiarity might have given way to carelessness; or the people might have taken for granted the holy presence of God and the ritual, and thus it would have become a mechanical performance. But when the great Day of Atonement came around, and the people saw that even the tabernacle had to be cleansed because of their impurities, they would realize the urgent necessity for them to examine their own souls before God. This should warn Christians today that church attendance, listening to preaching, and "hard work" at the church can become a humdrum round of activity, even if these things are done by genuine believers. There is need for a periodical examination of the heart before the Lord and a recognition that even at our best we lack in so many ways. Every now and then we should seek for a fresh filling of the Spirit of God and should ask God for His forgiveness for the many times we have failed Him.

Once again we are reminded that in the ministry of atonement within the Holy of Holies, Aaron had to do this alone (v. 17). One can imagine the feelings of the rest of the priests and people alike in their sense of the awe of God. This experience, too, became an appeal for a soul search as to their relationship with this holy God. We see also an aspect of the ministry which our High Priest, Jesus the Messiah, eventually performed for us. Of course, there was never any question as to whether Christ would be accepted by the Father. Yet we are told that Jesus, too, entered on our behalf before God (Heb. 9:24). But while the Levitical high priest had to repeat this ritual year by year, Jesus did this for us only once. We can rejoice in this great ministry that has made us accepted in the Beloved and has made us part of His family; we also wait eagerly for Christ to emerge the second time from the heavenly sanctuary, as Aaron did from the earthly one, for that great union with Him.

Atonement for altar

Having finished his duties within the tabernacle, the high priest went out to make atonement for the altar of burnt offering (v. 18). He and other priests continually ministered at this altar, and it also had to be cleansed because of the imperfection of the priests. Here, also, the sacrifices of the people were offered up, and since these represented an imperfect people, the altar also had to be purified. Taking some of the blood of the bull and of the goat, the high priest put it on the horns of the altar. Again the blood, representing the possibility of new life for both priests and people, was applied to the altar. So as to underscore perfect cleansing, the high priest sprinkled some more blood seven times on the altar so that it was consecrated for renewed service for another year. This action was a sign to the people that they needed the new life provided symbolically for them by the sacrifice of the goat; if individuals recognized the lesson of the exchange-of-life, they received a new life provided for them by God Himself through the ministry of the Holy Spirit.

The scapegoat

After this procedure the high priest took the live goat, and on behalf of the sons of Israel he confessed their sins upon the goat (v. 21). The goat then became sin and was led out into the wilderness by someone selected for the occasion. The great and precious lesson God wanted His people to learn was that after the sacrifice of the bull of the sin offering for the high priest and the goat of the sin offering for the community, the people could have full assurance that their sins had been taken away from them; never would they be confronted by their sins again (v. 22). A number of views have been suggested as to what the name of this goat, called ʿazaʾzel in Hebrew, stood for: the place to which the animal was sent or the name of a demon to which a ransom was possibly offered are two views. These ideas are inadequate and do no justice to the basic lesson of necessary atonement for sin and its forgiveness given through these two goats.

Believers today must not have the idea that the godly remnant in the days of the Mosaic constitution did not have the assurance that their sins were forgiven. God intended for them to know that if they believed in the exchange-of-life principle, they could *know* that they were saved. Any believer, watching the scapegoat taking away his sins, in a sense, understood well that he would never need to face his sins again. No wonder David testified that his sins were removed from him as far as the east is from the west (Ps. 103:12). If it were possible to measure the distance between east and west, then David would have found his sins; obviously this is an impossibility, and therefore David had perfect assurance that his sins had been taken from him. It is true that One was yet to come who would ratify at a point in history the significance of all the offerings of the days of the Old Testament king-dom by His one unique sacrifice; but this fact should never be construed to suggest that Old Testament believers did not have full assurance of forgiveness.

It is interesting to note also that the one who had led the goat out into the wilderness could not return directly into the midst of the community (v. 26). Because of his association with the community's sins, he had to wash his clothes and bathe his body in order to be ritually clean before coming back among the people.

C. Burnt Offering and Dedication

Right relationship with the Lord did not stop with atonement. Once this had been made, the high priest, the other priests, and the people could then enter into the blessedness of dedication to God.

After serving in humble clothes, the high priest went into the Holy Place in the tabernacle and took off his linen garments, leaving them there. After bathing in a specially prepared area, he put on his full regalia of clothing of glory and beauty, to then offer the ram of burnt offering for himself and the ram of burnt offering for the people. Serving in his clothes of glory as the official high priest after full atonement had been made, he could present himself and the nation before God in consecration for the new year.

In the prescribed manner the fat of the sin offerings was burned on the altar. But since the blood of these offerings had been offered in the Holy of Holies, a selected man took the remaining portions of the bull and the goat sin offerings to a place outside of the camp and burned them—hides, flesh, and refuse (v. 27)—because none of this was to be eaten. The one involved in this task had to wash his clothes and bathe his body with water before entering the camp. He had been in contact with the iniquities of the priests and the nation and had to cleanse himself before coming again among the elect people of God.

D. Day of Atonement Emphasis

It was impressed upon Israel that this day was the most important day of the year, occurring in the seventh month of their religious calendar, perhaps indicating that this month was the most perfect time for redemption and reconciliation for everyone (v. 29–30). The observance of this day was to be a permanent statute (vv. 29, 34), showing that the matter of atonement was an eternal principle on behalf of sinful man, although within the Mosaic constitution atonement was as yet imperfectly manifested. Later on, when the Messiah took the place of the high priest and fulfilled the various sacrifices, especially the sin offering, atonement was ratified in His person.

The Israelites were told to make this day a sabbath of solemn rest and a time when they were to afflict their souls (v. 31). This came to mean a day of fasting, prayer, and intense searching of soul. It is interesting to note that on no other religious day was there the call for an affliction of soul. Even when Israel lost her temples, the people of Israel never forgot this day, and in the development of the Jewish religion after the destruction of the Herodian Temple in A.D. 70, this day took on even greater meaning. There is tragedy in the current attempt to have a Day of Atonement without the shedding of the blood of a sin offering. While repentance, prayer, and good deeds, used by the Jewish people today as a substitute for the ritual of Leviticus 16 demonstrate a search for God, they are not enough to effect atonement for sin. May God help us to see this basic truth and also to see that instead of an animal Jesus the Messiah and Redeemer is now the great Sin Offering.

E. The Importance of Blood Atonement (17:1–16)

With its emphasis upon the blood, the Day of Atonement was the very heart of the sacrificial system of the Mosaic constitution. One can readily see the significance of the blood of the Antitype, Jesus the Messiah. The blood atonement completed by Jesus at Calvary was the very heart of Jesus' ministry and related to the fulfillment of all five sacrifices (chs. 1–5). But before considering this further, let us look at the Lord's instructions concerning the place where sacrifices were to be made.

Place of sacrifice (17:1–10)

In discussing the place where sacrifices were to be made, it is also necessary to refer to Deuteronomy 12. Before the Israelites ever entered the land, they were carefully instructed not to confuse their worship with the false worship of the people of the land. From archaeological finds and even from what Scripture declares we know that the inhabitants of the land were involved in a worship system which was not only false but also revoltingly unethical and immoral. The worship of idols in the land and the worship of Israel's God were to be kept separate to prevent Israel from becoming entangled with the abominations associated with false worship. As God's witnesses they were to have nothing to do with Canaanite worship and practice. The cup of iniquity of the people of the land was already full, and judgment was to fall on them; Israel was to possess their land (Gen. 15:16). Since Israel's God was the one true God, other people had to come to Him. Israel was not to turn to other gods because of the danger of losing a sensitivity to God's revelation and His requirements.

The Israelites were told that when they went into the land to possess it, the Lord would designate the place where sacrifices were to be offered (Deut. 12:5–6) until the temple was built. There were a number of sanctuary sites at different times, each sanctioned by the Lord: Bethel, Shiloh, etc. But at any place not sanctioned, Israelites were not permitted to sacrifice so that they would be prevented from straying toward Canaanite shrines. Therefore, blood guiltiness was ascribed to any person who slaughtered an ox, a lamb, or a goat as a sacrifice at an undesignated place, in or outside the camp (Lev. 17:3–4). The penalty for not listening to this command was separation from the people of Israel.

Perhaps the reader might again feel that this penalty was too harsh, but it always is a serious thing not to listen to God's clear instructions (v. 2). We might suggest three reasons for the severity of the penalty. First, God wanted His people to learn the correct way in which to worship Him. They were not to take things into their own hands concerning their approach to God. If they did, their call as a people would be in jeopardy, they would miss the meaning of atonement, and they could not be the witnesses God intended them to be.

Second, the people were reminded that God wanted them to be separated from the idolatrous systems of the other peoples of the Middle East, especially the situation in the land of Canaan. Instead of sacrificing in the fields wherever they chose and running the danger of contamination by pagan places of worship, God instructed His people not to bring their sacrifices to any cultic place (Deut. 12:13), nor were they to offer their sacrifices to the goat idols, associated with demons (Lev. 17:7). Rather, they were to destroy the false places of worship and the different images and idols. The Lord designated their place of worship and sacrifice until the time that the temple was built (Deut. 12:5, 6, 11, 12, 14). The positive value within these commands guarded against a misapplication of the great spiritual truths the Lord wanted His people to learn. This lesson has not been superseded but still stands today: if we are going to learn spiritual values, we must avoid compromising situations.

Finally, the penalty served as a warning to the people to protect the lessons of type regarding sacrifice and worship. In the proper use of the blood the Israelite gained truths that pertained to his relationship to the Lord. To mishandle the blood of an animal designated for sacrifice was most reprehensible in the sight of God, as we shall soon see when we discuss blood atonement. Because of the sacredness of the blood, therefore, no one, neither Israelite nor alien, had the right to eat it in any way whatsoever (Lev. 17:10). Animals other than those presented for sacrifices could be killed for food in the camp. However, the blood was not to be eaten but poured out on the ground (Deut. 12:15–16). Also, animals caught in hunting and not used for sacrifices could be killed and eaten, but, again, the blood was to be poured out on the ground first (Lev. 17:13).

The type lesson found here was very important. It was essential that the people of Israel handle the blood of the animal sacrifices aright since precious lessons concerning the ministry of the Messiah were involved. God had intended that through the lessons of the sacrificial system the time would come when the people would be perfectly schooled in the ministry that the Messiah would perform in their midst. That this did not happen, for most Jews in the first century was tragic indeed; even the disciples had to be taught the rudiments of the sacrificial system, the meaning of the shedding of blood, and other types that were fulfilled in the Messiah's life and work (Luke 24:25ff.).

Lest we shake our heads at this state of affairs, let us humble ourselves in the light of what many professing Christians today do with the idea of the substitutionary atonement made by Jesus Christ. There are many professing Christians who will have nothing to do with the blood of Jesus Christ in relation to salvation, and this is reprehensible to God. No wonder the penalty for unbelief and disobedience was so severe in the days of the Old Testament; but it is no less severe in the teaching of the New Testament because apart from the blood atonement of Jesus Christ there is no possibility for fellowship with the Lord throughout eternity.

Importance of the blood (vv. 11, 14)

We now come to the reason why the blood atonement was the very heart of the sacrificial system. The key phrase in verse 11 is that "the life (Heb. *nephesh*) of a creature is in the blood." *Nephesh* is here translated "life," and we are to understand that it is the blood that gives life to the body. When the blood of any creature is poured out, it describes a life given up. The rest of the verse takes on a deeper meaning: "It is the blood that makes atonement for one's life *(nephesh)*." The blood of an animal (representing its life) given in sacrifice was offered on the altar and was seen by God as atonement in the provision of a new life, including not just man's physical life but also his inner being. It was the sin nature of a person that made the death of a substitute necessary. It was the life of a substitute that was given to a person; it was blood applied to the altar that God saw as interposed between Himself and a person. This was atonement!

We shall not discuss here the question of whether God could have made man's redemption possible in another way, or whether blood was necessary for salvation! It is interesting to note that this was a question which intrigued some leaders in the church in the Middle Ages. However, our purpose here is to ascertain what God was saying in the Levitical system by our employing sound hermeneutics, by our relating a type fulfillment to the ministry of Jesus the Messiah, and by our noting the application of blood atonement today.

Perhaps the meaning of blood atonement can be seen in the record concerning Adam and Eve and the steps God took to restore them. What was the remedy that God announced to Adam and Eve that would reverse at least the tragedy of spiritual separation? It is the author's opinion that God chose the most vivid means to underscore the wrong choice our parents made with its terrible consequences. The Scripture does not tell us of the encounter God had with our first parents in teaching this method. We *do* know that the life of an animal was taken so that Adam and Eve could be clothed (Gen. 3:21) and also that Cain and Abel had some knowledge of the means of redemption through blood atonement.

What was involved in the killing of an animal (or animals) so that God could clothe Adam and Eve? No doubt God forcefully demonstrated to Adam what was involved in restoration. Adam and Eve died (spiritual separation from God and later, physical death) because of their wrong choices concerning the tree. Thus, for their restoration an animal had to die, a vivid reminder of the consequences of their wrong deeds. When our first parents confessed their sins (and we assume that they did), they had to see an animal's substitute death on an altar as the judgment for their disobedience. They had to recognize the death of the animal in the light of *their own* deaths. But God was gracious as well as just. Not only did an animal die, with Adam and Eve in identification with it, but they also were able to receive life in what we have identified already as the exchange-of-life principle.

In the Levitical system then there was the reminder that a blood atonement was God's appointed method of restoration. An animal had to die, and its blood had to be applied in the specified manner. Blood and life are synonymous, and the blood applied in the proper places was the symbol of a new life. For this reason the blood was sacred. Also, atonement through shed blood conveyed great lessons. Because of all these reasons, no one was to eat blood of any kind, for such would be sacrilege. To misuse blood also meant a violation of the law, because the shedding of blood was a type of the death of Jesus the Messiah for sin and of the offer of a new life, which was linked to His blood.

For the ultimate restoration of Adam and Eve and of the whole human race all the animal deaths in every succeeding generation had to point to the One who would fulfill their significance and ratify people's faith in the exchange-of-life principle. Adam and Eve were thus instructed concerning their Redeemer. This was the substance of the first gospel message in Genesis 3:15, which called for the bruising of His heel, understood in the light of fuller revelation as the death of the Redeemer on God's appointed altar. It is interesting to note concerning Eve that she may have anticipated His coming in the birth of Cain (Gen. 4:1). Her pronouncement of Cain as the man, the Lord, could have been *her* expectation that *this* one indeed was to be Him who would supplant the prescribed animal sacrifices. At least her mind was set on the One who would provide life in place of death.

It is no different for us today. In Christ's death we see the penalty required for our sins if we die in our sinful state (Ezek. 18:4): "The soul who sins is the one who will die"). It is as if God is showing us, as He showed Adam and Eve, and as He showed Israel in the Levitical system, that redemption requires that we identify with the death of Another—our only means of restoration!

In a last word in Leviticus 17 God's mercy was extended to those who ate flesh of an animal that had died of itself or that had been torn by beasts. This would mean that the animal had not been killed in the manner prescribed, i.e., having its blood drained out on the ground. And it would mean that the person had eaten blood, an act absolutely forbidden by the law. However, if a person realized his error in partaking of blood, he had to regard himself as unclean, wash his clothes, and bathe in water; he was not ceremonially clean until evening (vv. 15–16). At least God did extend His mercy to one who perhaps unwittingly ate this kind of meat or to one who had second thoughts because of the severe penalty involved. However, if the person was so calloused that he had no respect for the blood, the harsh penalty, entirely justified then, was applied and the person had to bear the iniquity of his deed.

For Further Study

1. In a Bible dictionary or encyclopedia (see bibliography) read articles on: atonement, *'aza'zel* (scapegoat), Day of Atonement (festivals), mercy seat.

2. Based on the rationale for the Day of Atonement, is there value today for congregations to have a day or period of time every year for self-examination and spiritual emphasis?

3. Review the lessons of the assurance of the forgiveness of sin in connection with the scapegoat. Look for other Old Testament passages which also emphasize assurance (you might begin with Micah 7:18–20).

4. What is the problem of the shedding of Jesus' blood as the antitype when some people will minimize or delete the emphasis on the blood atonement in the Levitical system?

5. Some very traditional Jews on the eve of the Day of Atonement kill a rooster for a male and a hen for a female and swing them over the heads respectively of men and women who seek forgiveness for their sins. How do you explain this practice in view of how Judaism has structured itself to be a religion without a sacrifice?

Chapter 6

Laws of Morality
(Leviticus 18:1–20:34)

We come now to those laws regulating personal relationships among God's elect people. These too constituted an aspect of worship along with sacrifices, diet, cleanliness, and blood atonement. The Israelites were schooled in correct interpersonal behavior before they entered the Promised Land because they would be exposed to the corruption of the Canaanite life style. Archaeology has demonstrated the utter moral degradation of these inhabitants, and therefore Israel was warned to pursue a godly way of life absolutely opposed to that of the Canaanites. As God's elect people they were hedged with a number of negative moral restrictions (ch. 18). They were also provided with an expansion of the Ten Commandments that carefully underlined morals (ch. 19) and were cited penalties for violations of biblical principles (ch. 20).

A. Moral Principles (ch. 18)

God began His instructions by announcing, "I am the LORD your God" (v. 2). If Israel was to be the elect people of God, they were not to be caught in the crosscurrent of controversy between two spiritual systems, that of the Lord and that of the pagan gods. Each pagan system had its own set of "moral standards." For this reason Israel's God (the God of the whole universe and therefore sovereign over any supposed national deities) said to His people, "You must obey my laws and be careful to follow my decrees" (v. 4). And He also said, "You must not do as they do in Egypt, where you used to live, and you must not do as they do in the land of Canaan . . ." (v. 3). These restrictions were intended to protect the people from pagan moral standards that catered to lustful desires of unregenerate hearts. Sinners found it convenient to combine pagan worship and deviate moral practices. Israelites were exhorted not to fall into this trap. If the people obeyed the Lord, the holiness of God would be reflected in their morals, and they could expect to reap eternal life provided they adopted a proper attitude to God's Word (v. 5). If the Word of God was the Israelite's authority for moral standards, he could also recognize the place that atonement had in the Covenant.

Unlawful marriages (vv. 6-8)

Holy living was to be reflected in the proper selection of a mate. An acceptable husband or wife was not to be a close blood relative (v. 6). The Lord wanted to preserve an atmosphere of confidence and to show the limits of adultery (Exod. 20:14). Adultery was not only forbidden by the Mosaic Covenant; God has pronounced a universal commandment against it that is binding on the whole human race in every nation (i.e., Reuben's curse, Gen. 49:4; also see 1 Cor. 5:1).

Sexual relations by children with those near of kin, e.g., a mother, a stepmother, or even a stepmother who was a widow, were regarded as "uncovering the father's nakedness" (NASB). Even the pagan abhorred this kind of relation (1 Cor. 5:1) because of a glimmer in his conscience. The divine law, once given to the human race in its infancy, is still recognized by some pagans, although perverted in part because of the fallen nature of unbelievers.

Those near of kin also included sisters, either a full sister or a half sister (born to either father or mother) as well as granddaughters (vv. 9-11). Sexual relations with any of these kin were forbidden. If a widow remarried and had children, the daughters of the second marriage were still considered sisters to the mother's first family; therefore, there were to be no relations between sisters of the second family and any males of the first family.

Abraham is an interesting case because he married his half sister (Gen. 20:12). In this case there seemed to be divine sanction, but the law subsequently prohibited these relationships. The divine wisdom in these injunctions promoted domestic peace and discouraged licentiousness.

Near relations (vv. 12-14) also included aunts (both paternal and maternal), uncles and the wives of paternal uncles. Nephews were forbidden to marry their aunts, and vice versa, although nothing is said about uncles married to their neices. Neither is there anything said about marriage of cousins (see Num. 36:11). But, the Lord did not want confusion in families and He prohibited unchecked lust. Rather, the emphasis was upon forming increasing circles of chaste relationships for a wholesome atmosphere.

Injunctions also applied to proper relations of men to their daughters-in-law and their sisters-in-law (vv. 15–16). The law did make one exception to v. 16, in the practice of levirate marriages, i.e., in which a widow was taken as a wife by the brother of the deceased *when the deceased had left no (son)*. This exception allowed family lines to be preserved and inheritances to remain unbroken. It was considered a tragedy for a man to be without children, thereby cutting off the continuity of his line, e.g., Ruth having had no children from Mahlon (Ruth 4:10). While there were times when a particular brother could not do this service for a deceased brother because of legal entanglements, yet someone in the family needed to take the widow as his wife so there could be children in the name of the deceased. She had the right to shame her brother-in-law in public for his despicable action if he would not marry her (Deut. 25:5–10). In general, however, daughters-in-law were to be regarded as daughters and sisters-in-law were to be seen as sisters because the Lord intended that there be an affection between relatives and a high regard for dignity in the social fabric.

It was regarded as gross wickedness for a man to be involved with both a woman and her daughter or with a woman and her granddaughter (v. 17).

There were instructions to curb an aspect of polygamy. One was not to be married to a woman and also take her sister for a wife while the first was still alive, thereby creating rivalry (v. 18). The most famous situation like this concerned Jacob, Leah, and Rachel. The Lord here expressed His concern for the personal feelings of individuals, not wanting a situation to arise in which there would be domestic problems between wives and the husband, e.g., 1 Samuel 1:6–7.

People have wondered whether the Lord sanctioned polygamy during the patriarchal stage, while laws given later prohibited it. Jesus, in commenting on the aspect of divorce, stated that in the beginning, i.e., when Adam and Eve were in the state of innocence, the ideal was one wife for a husband (Matt. 19:8). We do note instances of polygamy, e.g., Jacob, Samuel's father, David, etc. among the people of Israel. However, over a period of time polygamy was gradually abandoned since the law condemned it.

Unlawful lust (vv. 19–30)

A number of injunctions appear in verses 19 to 30 that put a hedge about the elect people to curb their lusts and to encourage godly living, reflecting the holiness of the Lord. We live in a day when our society has abandoned absolute standards of morality, following, rather, an ideology of relativity and permissiveness, especially in sexual relations. The only criterion for having sexual relations seems to be the feelings one person has for another. If there is some kind of "love" between a fellow and a girl, the criterion of relativity permits the two to engage in sexual relations. What our society will ultimately learn, when the whirlwind is reaped, is that permissiveness has its price tag: broken health, broken spirits or severe, psychological disturbances, unwanted children, family crises, and perhaps a frightful loss of life in abortion. We will learn the hard way that God has woven His absolute standards into the fabric of the world of men. God never intended these laws to be harsh; rather, the Lord wanted man, His highest creation, to enjoy life, family, children, and society in ways that bring joy to the heart rather than grief and sorrow. Therefore, God cared for His people Israel and wanted to create an island of godliness and desirable morality in the Middle East that would attract the pagans to something better than what they had. These laws are for our guidance likewise.

First of all, it was not permitted for a husband to approach his wife at the time of her period (v. 19; see also ch. 15). Furthermore, God anticipated the strong temptations some Israelites would have when viewing the moral practices of the Canaanites and warned the people of Israel not to imitate these moral deviates. No one was to have intercourse with a neighbor's wife (v. 20; Exod. 20:17). It was absolutely forbidden to offer children to Molech in sacrifice (to pass them through the fire) to gain some spiritual favor or blessing (v. 21); the Lord called this practice a profanation of His name.

Neither was there to be any homosexuality (including lesbianism), an *abomination* to His holiness (v. 22). In addition, it was moral perversion to be involved sexually with animals. Safeguards were given to secure the peace and purity of human society and to provide optimum conditions for learning spiritual lessons of salvation and godly development.

Another theme concerned possession of the land of Canaan (vv. 24–28) as this possession related to moral living. Canaan had been promised to Abraham and his descendants when they would return from slavery in a foreign land (Gen. 15:13ff.). This would be in a day when the iniquity of the land's inhabitants would be full; and ultimately, when the Canaanites did not repent from their horrible sins, they were judged by the Lord. Condemnation came through invasion and death by the Israelites. It was, however, the iniquity of the Canaanites that had defiled the land (v. 25), and in judgment the land spewed out its inhabitants. The land could not endure nor even bear their gross violations. The Israelites were also warned that they were not to be involved in the kinds of sins in which the Canaanites were enmeshed; and if the elect people did not drive out the Canaanites, if they were not obedient to the Lord's standards, there was a danger that the Israelites would suffer the same fate. Even today, deviations in the morals of a people make the land cry out because of the foul sins it is compelled to bear.

When individual cases of moral deviation occurred, the punishment that was to be applied was separation from the people of God (see also ch. 20). Holy living would insure peace and safety and would, at the same time, also provide a witness to other countries and peoples of the Middle East. Many individuals from other nations would then be encouraged to enter the Commonwealth of Israel and share in that people's special relationship with the Lord. It was a serious thing, therefore, to go against the Word of God so as to profane His name. Not only would the people suffer personally if they did, but the plan of God would become temporarily blunted.

B. The Ten Commandments and Other Regulations (ch. 19)

Chapter 19 provides a further explanation of the Ten Commandments and a call to holiness—God's holiness (v. 2). This was not an impossible life style for those who were spiritually regenerate because the ministry of the Holy Spirit made possible the Spirit-filled life. Those people who had problems with the moral standards would realize that they needed an atonement for their sins when they understood that they had broken them. Furthermore, God spoke directly and appealingly to His people, asking them to follow Him as their Father in a godly life style.

Once again the people were reminded that they were to reverence both mother and father (v. 3). Respect for our parents leads to respect for the Lord, and the latter is made easier when the child is taught to respect his parents and their authority. This has never been abrogated, for in the New Testament Paul calls this the first commandment with promise (Eph. 6:2).

Right on the heels of this commandment came the reminder that the people were to keep the Sabbaths (Lev. 19:3). The seventh day of rest was important not only for people but also for animals and land. No matter what political regime or social system is embraced, it is soon apparent that there is a need for the body to rest and for the mind to relax. The Law provided the seventh day of the week, while the church observes the first day of the week. The principle is that one day be set aside for worship. Both the Old and the New Covenants teach that rest and relaxation are to include the spiritual facet, which will develop the inner man.

To emphasize the importance of these two instructions for holiness and other instructions as well this characteristic formula was uttered by God: "I am the LORD your God" (v. 3). This was, in a sense, the signature of the One who initiated these instructions; it is given fifteen times in this chapter to communicate His authority. The Father, as the Head of His family, Israel, communicated His will and wanted His people to be obedient to His Word. We today are even more obligated to listen to God than they were since we have a greater revelation of His will than they did.

Israel was warned not to make idols nor to make molten gods so as to worship them (v. 4), thereby dividing loyalties in their worship; for the Lord is a jealous God (Josh. 24:19). This is not meant in the sense that a young man may be jealous over his fiancee's feelings. The jealousness of God is an aspect of His holiness; He could not sanction worship of the gods of Canaan, in whose names so many vile deeds had been perpetrated. Holiness is to be seen as the positive essence of the personality of the Supreme Being, and the elect people were never to be confused as to the character of their Father. Our Lord also reminds us today that we should never be divided in our interests.

Instructions were repeated concerning the feast of the sacrifice of peace offerings (vv. 5-8), already discussed in 7:15-18. Probably the reasons for mentioning it here were twofold: 1) These peace offerings constituted an example of one important regulation, e.g., no flesh was to be eaten on the third day after the sacrifice was made. Obedience demonstrated a positive, wholesome respect for the Word of God. 2) When a person offered such a peace offering, it encouraged others to do likewise and to enter into a spontaneous expression of gratitude for the blessings of a beneficent Father.

God also directed the farmer to care for the less fortunate (vv. 9–10), e.g., he was not to wholly reap the corners or edges of the fields or pick up what fell from the gleanings during reaping. Fallen fruit or what was not in clusters, e.g., fallen grapes of the vineyard, were to be left on the ground. There would be enough for the owners of the fields in the harvest, and they were not to be selfish or greedy; by providing for the needy, the owners would have the opportunity to show kindness and liberality, e.g., the story of Boaz and Ruth.

Boaz's generosity was blessed of the Lord in that He gave him the desires of his heart.

The Law laid down social and economic principles on behalf of the poor, the needy, and strangers. But one thing the Law did not do; the poor were not encouraged to feel that the nation owed them a living. While the poor had provisions set aside for them, they had to expend some effort in order to obtain their food; the Mosaic Covenant never fostered the concept of "getting something for nothing." While societies today have a responsibility to the poor and needy, every effort and use of imagination should be expended to keep these people occupied so that their sustenance is never received as part of a system in which nothing is expected in return.

In civil transactions—business, trade, etc.—it was absolutely forbidden to engage in theft, dishonesty, and all kinds of lies (vv. 11–12). Trying to verify a lie through an appeal to God's name was condemned. Believers today should have a tender conscience when they are dealing with the people of the world. Men of the world will steal, deal falsely, and lie; not so the Christian! The latter is to hold to a standard of integrity and righteousness, knowing he lives as if he stands in the presence of God. It is only in this way that many in the world will be confronted with real godliness.

Neither was one to oppress or defraud his neighbor, including the withholding of wages from an employee (v. 13; see also Exod. 22:7–15, 21–27). Israelites were to live with one another as one big family, and each was to respect his neighbor's person and property. The Law enjoined mutual trust among the populace so that property would be safe under any circumstances; there were penalties to correct any breach of trust, especially for the poor person (Deut. 24:15). In all of these situations we learn guides for today's living. Christians indeed should live with each other as a family with no fear of any questionable conditions, and certainly Christian employers should be scrupulously honest in the payment of wages.

We live in a world of imperfections, and it is unfortunate when people born into this world have defects that prevent them from functioning like normal human beings (Lev. 19:14). It was a gross injustice to curse a deaf person because he caused some inconvenience. Neither was anything to be placed before a blind person to cause him harm. Men can be hard-hearted, but God expected His people as a family to help those less fortunate.

A double standard of justice was to be avoided (v. 15). The man of standing and the rich man were not to be flattered; neither was the poor man to receive any special consideration because of his condition. Total impartiality was to be the standard. God is just, and the Law is likewise, encouraging people to live in His light and to reflect His justice. Justice and integrity within the church should prevail as in the law of Moses.

Slander of any kind (vv. 16--18) could not be countenanced. A later interpretation of the law demonstrated that when one slandered, three people were killed: the one being slandered, the one engaged in slandering, and the one hearing the slander. This evil of slander twists every moral fiber of a person. The New Testament declares that the wrong use of the tongue defiles the entire body (James 3:6).

Slander could lead to arguments, and even the murder of a neighbor (Lev. 19:16); grievances were never to be settled in a fight. Furthermore, within the family of Israel no one was to harbor hatred for anyone (v. 17). Certainly one could reprove his neighbor with a heartfelt concern by telling him where he was at fault. This is not prying into other people's lives; instead, when Israelites took an interest in their neighbors, it had a good effect upon the entire community. On the other hand, hatred can lead only to vengeance or grudge bearing against one's neighbor and to the disruption of peace in the community (v. 18). Godly relations with neighbors are also an imperative in the body of Christ, and we are given specific commands to put away all bitterness, rage and anger, brawling and slander, along with every form of malice; we are to be kind and compassionate to one another, forgiving each other, just as we have been forgiven (Eph. 4:31–32).

The heart of all neighbor relations and, in fact, of the Law, was the statement ["You shall] love your neighbor as yourself" (Lev. 19:18).

The law was never heartless, coldly legalistic, or characterized by an untouchable holiness; too many people think of it in these terms. Even Jesus, Who lived as a Jew under the law, reminded His generation that the first rule was to love the Lord and that the second was to love one's neighbor as one's self, principles that were not new insofar as Jesus was concerned. They were already being emphasized among the religious leaders of the house of Hillel. Jesus' ministry was to turn His generation back to the Scriptures and away from the confusing combination of Scripture and many of the man-made traditions then prevalent. Jesus emphasized a proper respect for the written law (the Scriptures) with its encouragement to have a proper life style. Believers of the nation of Israel were to love each other as taught in the Law. The Christian can do no less. With a new nature and nurtured by Scripture, we too have a way to live godly. When there is a lack of love in the body of Christ, it hinders the preaching of the gospel to the world.

In living a sanctified life, nothing was trivial (vv. 19–25). So as to emphasize separation, the people were not to breed one kind of cattle with different kinds of cattle, nor sow two different seeds in the same field, nor mix two or more kinds of yarn, e.g., linen and wool woven together in the same garment. God promised abundantly to bless both physically and materially in every way as a testimony to the pagans, but Israel never was to copy their ways.

In cases of sexual immorality between a master and a female slave (when the woman was engaged to another man but had not yet been bought out of slavery), the death penalty was waived (vv. 20–22), perhaps for various reasons. She could have been frightened by a master's authority, or he may have been ignorant of the slave girl's betrothal, etc. Yet, whatever the reasons, there was no escape from a penalty for him; he had to publicly offer a guilt offering. The law was completely impartial so that the authorities were considerate of the girl, when taking account of her circumstances.

The people were not to eat of newly planted fruit trees for the first three years (vv. 23–25), and in the fourth year all fruit was to be considered the Lord's and dedicated to Him as an act of thanksgiving. From the fifth year on the people could eat of these trees. This exhibition of patience was a testimony of love and care as well as a curb on a greedy appetite. Again the restriction is repeated concerning eating anything containing blood (v. 26).

In addition, divination and sorcery were expressly forbidden

(v. 26). It was a travesty to seek guidance from questionable sources when, in fact, Israel possessed a revelation from their God who was the God of the whole universe. Considering times as being "lucky" or "unlucky" apart from asking the Lord about matters was taboo. The people's guidance and safety lay in simple reliance on the Lord.

The side-growths of the head were not to be rounded, and the edges of the beard were not to be harmed (v. 27). The religious custom of some of the pagans was to cut their hair and beards in certain ways to honor their gods. Even in these details the people of God were not to conform to the heathen customs of the land. Neither were the Israelites to cut their bodies in any way to show grief for any deceased loved ones, nor mar their bodies with any tattoo marks (v. 28), also heathen practices. Israel was to be loyal to God's word. On so solemn an occasion as the funeral of a fellow Israelite there were to be no demonstrations of grief involving mutilation of the body. Tears could be expected, but trust in and consolation from the word of God were to be the primary means of comfort.

Israelite daughters were never to become prostitutes, especially when persuaded to do so by their fathers (v. 29). Unfortunately, the Canaanite religion with its fertility cult offered a terrible temptation; yet under the law God held Israelite parents responsible for their daughters' welfare and commanded that they be provided a better and more blessed way. This is still good instruction for believers today. The parents' first concern for daughters should not be material advantage through marrying them into well-to-do families. Instead, parents should seek to direct daughters to the mates of God's choice.

Sabbaths and the sanctuary (the tabernacle) were to be revered (v. 30), which meant that there was to be no "business as usual" on these days. Keeping the Sabbath holy was the heartbeat of the spiritual standing of the nation. If the Lord's house and worship were to be abandoned, the nation would fall into evil; and this is still true. The real strength of a nation is developed when believers worship regularly in the Lord's house. If spiritual devotion is neglected, the nation can only go downhill.

Contact with mediums and spiritists was regarded as defiling (v. 31). To seek information from these sources could mean only a complete lack of trust in the Lord and His Word. The Lord will not share time with Satan's kingdom. Satan is clever, and he can provide, through willing mediums, some extraordinary communication. The

New Testament confirms this when it describes Satan as an angel of light and his servants as people who are disguised as servants of righteousness (2 Cor. 11:14, 15). Israel was warned not to be involved with this method of gaining information, and Christians are also warned today to avoid spiritists altogether.

One must show reverence for the gray-headed person and extend honor to the aged as a sign of respect for wisdom (v. 32). The elders held the leadership of the people, and there was an emphasis upon their earthly authority and wisdom, which was to serve as a guide to respect for the authority and commandments of the Lord. Perhaps we have had such an emphasis on the cult of youth in recent years that we have forgotten the premium that God places on the elderly in the social structure. It is wrong to retire people when they are in their prime or to neglect those from whom society can still benefit.

People of non-Israelite origin who chose to make their homes among Israelites were to be encouraged, loved, and treated as the native Israelite (vv. 33, 34). One of the purposes of the law was to attract pagans and bring them to the knowledge of the truth of the God of all the earth, e.g., Ruth and a host of others like her. Into the Commonwealth of Israel the stranger was to be accepted, and when accepted, no question was to be raised as to his country of origin. In much the same way today believers should exhibit kindness to non-Christians for the purpose of gaining them for the Redeemer.

The last instructions in chapter 19 applied to day-to-day economic matters (vv. 35, 36). Use of weights and balances for trade in the market and for payment for work on the land demanded of men absolute integrity. While Israel in Egypt had been defrauded of their remuneration, God reminded them that they should not do to one another what the Egyptians had done to them. Israelites, because they were all considered a family, were to treat one another with consideration and respect, and nothing would be so degrading as not to be fair in every business exchange. God's instructions today likewise enjoin us to lay aside *every* falsehood and to not steal any more (Eph. 4:25, 28).

This exposition of the commandments closed with a reminder that the Israelites were to observe all of God's decrees and all His laws and were to *follow* them (v. 37). The law made Israel distinct from all the other peoples on earth, and to the glory of God many from among the nations were attracted to righteousness and entered Israel's ranks in Old Testament times. There have been times since then in the history of the church when many have come to the Lord because the church has lived faithfully by His Word. But there have been and are now times when the church has wandered far from what she should be, and this has caused a loss in her testimony to the world.

C. The Penalties for Violating Moral Principles (20:1-27)

In this chapter the Law specified various penalties for violating the moral regulations of chapters 18 and 19. Instructions and regulations without penalties are nothing more than good advice, but when penalties are attached, it is possible to enforce the regulations when they are broken. It was God's intention to rid the land of the Canaanites and to cleanse it of their hideous, immoral, and ungodly life styles; He wanted His people to be very careful not to pollute themselves, lest they suffer the same penalty the Canaanites suffered. (v. 22).

Even as the first commandment reminded the people to have no other gods before them, Israelites were warned about the god Molech. Molech was one of the Middle Eastern deities, whose image was that of a red hot, glowing, bronze figure with arms stretched out to receive children offered to it. Child sacrifice to this deity represented a perverted and twisted idea of a hellish, tyrannical consecration, but this supposed worship was an antithesis of what Israel's God desired in His love. The penalty under the Law for perverted worship was death, and the people were to stone the offender. The Lord also cut such an offender off from His people because this evil idolatry defiled His sanctuary and profaned His holy name (vv. 2-3). The penalty was severe to prevent the spread of idolatry in Israel; let such an activity start with just one person, and an entire community might be led astray.

The Lord warned the people not to become apathetic in punishing an offender for his idolatry (vv. 4-5). In fact, the Lord would hold apathetic leaders as accomplices if they refused to punish an offender exactly as God commanded. The Lord would severely punish anyone who failed to heed and obey His Word, both a man and his household. If the law was to be a schoolmaster to teach the high and exalted nature of God and the wickedness of substituting another deity for Him, then flouting the divinely given ordinances had to incur severe penalties. God wants man to learn loving submission; yet, there are times when the lessons must be painfully learned in the school of hard discipline.

A person who sought mediums and spiritists to gain spiritual guidance was breaking the first commandment (v. 6). Israel was to have no other counselors but the Lord; any other would only lead the people astray. Again the penalty was severe: the stoning to death of such twisted people because bloodguiltiness was upon them (v. 27). God will never bless people, especially believers, who turn to questionable sources of authority and thereby make God into a liar.

People were encouraged to consecrate themselves and to show themselves holy before the Lord (v. 7). This was stated in the form of a preface to what was coming regarding penalties for gross moral laxity. People often see the God of the Old Testament as a stern disciplinarian without any compassion. But Israel as a people knew that the Lord had set His love on them, even though they were of a limited number, and had redeemed them out of Egypt. He wanted to guide them, so He gave them His Word, in which He perfectly combined love and discipline as a clear indication that He cared for them. Therefore, God called Israel to a holiness that required their willingness to practice the life style indicated in His decrees, or His Word (v. 8). God's holiness has never changed, and we, likewise, are to show ourselves holy to the Lord.

A most heinous sin was to curse one's father or mother. To do so amounted to a denial of the parents who gave them life; yes, even the body of the ungrateful offender was actually a gift of the father and mother. The law called for the death penalty for such a defiant son (or daughter) because of the sin of bloodguiltiness. There was no sacrifice in the sacrificial system that removed this guilt. The penalty was severe for two reasons: 1) Cursing in the ancient sense involved using the name of some deity who brought evil upon the one being cursed. For a son to curse his parents meant he did this by the name of some other deity, thereby acknowledging the authority of another God instead of the true God. 2) The son called into question his obedience to his earthly parents, through whom he was to learn to obey the heavenly Father. Paul called the fifth commandment the first one with a promise, for it promised obedient and faithful children long life on earth (Eph. 6:2, 3). Christian families should strive for close, meaningful relationships; there ought to be no generation gap. Even in cases of the families of young Christians, when one or both parents are unbelievers, the believers are responsible before the Lord to so live in their relationships to their parents that they can be won to the Lord.

Moral guidelines concerning proper family relationships were previously specified (ch. 18), but here in chapter 20 the penalties for moral laxity were fixed (vv. 10–21). The penalties were drastic. The death penalty by stoning was required for both parties in various situations of adultery (vv. 10–12), in homosexuality, (v. 13), and in cases of human-animal relationships (vv. 15–16). A most severe death penalty was reserved for a man marrying a woman and her mother for sexual purposes (v. 14): all three, after being executed, were to be burned with fire, that is, burning the corpse after death.

Both parties were cut off from fellowship with the people of God, i.e., suffered death, when a man involved himself with his sister or half sister (v. 17) and when one lay with a woman during her period (v. 18). The punishment for a man taking a blood aunt was for both to bear their guilt, i.e., God Himself would see to the matter (v. 19). Finally, in cases where one took either his uncle's wife or his brother's wife, the penalty was childlessness, a keen disappointment in a society that put such a premium on children. God wanted to protect the Israelites from the gross Canaanite sins and to demonstrate the deepest meaning of family life that would be the foundation for the best possible society. The principles which upheld these laws were never repealed with the inception of the New Testament, thereby insuring continuous, stabilized societies for those who will use them.

Obedience to the Law meant that the land would be blessed, while disregard for the word was tantamount to defiling the land. The land had spewed out the Canaanites because they disregarded a basic morality; Israel was to be distinctive in their love for the Law so that in this very land they would be a blessing for the whole earth (vv. 22–24). Ultimately in that land there would be the salvation ministry of Jesus the Messiah and the Redeemer that would have meaning for all peoples.

While no specific penalty was attached for disobeying the dietary laws, disobedience in these matters could only lead to more serious difficulties. Samson was not immediately penalized for taking honey from the carcass of a dead lion (Judg. 14:8, 9), a definite uncleanness since he touched a dead body when he was a Nazarite. Yet this wrong plus other wrongs set up a pattern that finally led to his telling the Philistines the source of his strength (Judg. 16:17). This story is a fitting conclusion to Leviticus 20, which described penalties that followed wrongdoing when God's word was disregarded.

For Further Study

1. In a Bible dictionary or encyclopedia (see bibliography) read articles on: adultery, commandments (ten), crime and punishment for homosexuality, idolatry, lust, morals, sex.

2. Review again and make a list of what is considered as 1) lawful marriage contributing to morally correct family ties and 2) unlawful marriage.

3. Is there a way today to balance the condemnation of the practice of homosexuality and the pastoral ministry to the homosexual?

4. Christians often live as a minority in a community. Do they have a right to strive for and vote through laws which commit the community to moral standards in business, Sunday observance, and care for the disadvantaged?

5. List a number of reasons why the occult (seeking guidance from mediums, etc.) was a deadly peril to Israel. Are there parallels today for the body of Christ?

6. Get a concordance and look for the word "love" in the Old Testament in connection with love for God or for man. Can this be a background for what Jesus taught (Mark 12:30–31)?

Chapter 7

Laws Pertaining to Priesthood
(Leviticus 21:1–22:33)

In these two chapters Moses instructed the priests as to their manner of living and serving in a way that would inspire the people to learn the meaning of holiness. Even the sacrifices that the people brought were to be under the scrutiny of the priests, who guided Israel in the worship of their God.

A. Priesthood Service (21:1–22:16)

In this chapter the priest is, in a sense, an overseer of the community. He was not expected to mourn for deaths among the people (vv. 1–5), only for the relatives closest to him, e.g., mother, father, son, daughter, brother, and unmarried sister; and perhaps he would not even mourn his wife since Ezekiel was prohibited from mourning for the passing of his wife (Ezek. 24:16–18). The continuity of ministry had to be maintained, so the priest was spared from as much contact with the dead as possible because such contact defiled him temporarily. Yet, as the priests ministered to their people, they came to know their heartaches and joys. They were encouraged to have compassion and yearning for them, while they didn't reveal all their feelings. This is a pattern of procedure for ministers today.

The Jewish priests were not to shave their heads, nor the edges of their beards, nor make any cuts in their flesh (v. 5) so as to imitate the signs of mourning among heathen peoples of the Middle East (19:27–28). It was the priests' distinctive privilege to offer the food of their God (meaning food and meat) in His presence, and a wrong example would leave a bad representation of the Lord Himself for the people of Israel (v. 6).

The priest was not to take a questionable woman for a wife, i.e., one defiled by prostitution (v. 8), lest it would reflect on the priest's service and his relationship with the Lord (vv. 8–9). The priest was not to marry a divorcee either, and while the law did permit the bill of divorcement (Deut. 24:1–4), the priest's choice of a mate was to reflect the ideal estate of our first parents in their innocence and therefore be an example. When speaking of divorce, Jesus referred to Adam and Eve (Matt. 19:8). The figure of the church as the pure bride of Christ, representative of an ideal marriage, also comes to mind (Eph. 5:22–33).

Horrifying indeed was the situation where a priest's daughter became a prostitute (v. 9). She not only defiled herself, but her father's house and ministry were also involved. The Law, in order to prevent loss of influence for the things of God, called for retribution: after execution the daughter was to be burned with fire as a judgment of God, although in some family situations the erring daughter was driven out instead. The fifth commandment was and is a God-instituted law which cannot be broken without serious consequences.

The high priest, having been consecrated and instructed to wear the garments of his exalted office (v. 10), could not bring into question the symbols of his position, e.g., by mourning, even for his father or mother (v. 11); by uncovering his head and tearing his hair; or by leaving the sanctuary to mourn with others while in ministry (vv. 10, 12). The sanctuary was not to be defiled thereby.

The bride of the high priest had to be an unmarried woman, a virgin of his own people (vv. 13–15). He was never to marry a divorcee or even a woman who was a widow; obviously he was never to have for a wife one who had been defiled by prostitution. This strictness was intended to insure that his sons would not be disqualified for the office of high priest nor led astray by a bad example. The high priest was to perpetuate the ideal of a lasting marriage with the wife of one's youth. In a sense the marriage of a high priest was also the model of the relationship that existed between the nation and her God, by which Israel was regarded as the bride and God as the husband, e.g., in the setting of the Song of Solomon. One also sees the type fulfilled in the church and her Head—the church as the pure virgin (2 Cor. 11:2), holy and blameless (Ephs. 5:27), and Christ as the Bridegroom pledged to His bride.

Unfortunately, this life is marred by defects because of the presence of the curse upon nature, and it is a heartrending experience for parents to rear children with physical or mental defects. Especially would this be so for priests whose children might be affected when they would come to adulthood and seek to minister before the Lord (vv. 16–24). The priests who ministered had to be without a physical blemish and be free of defects such as blindness, lameness, disfigurement of the face, deformity in any limb, a crippled hand or foot, hunchbacked, dwarfness, defect in the eye, festering or running sores or damaged testicles, etc., that the altar not be defiled. The type consideration primarily concerned the messianic High Priest to come. As the priest had to be perfect in every way, so Jesus was in reality the perfect One. God however was gracious to priests who could not exercise their office because of some physical defect. They could eat of the bread of God (v. 22), e.g., of the holy things, meal offerings, wave offerings, peace offerings, and of the most holy things, the sin offerings. By partaking of the food from the sacrifices and even by having fellowship with other priests who *could* exercise their office, the priests with deformities could have full communion and fellowship with the Lord. In this way God never intended that earthly burdens be greater than men could bear. In the Resurrection, ultimately, believers will no longer have deformities.

Aaron and his descendants were also warned about handling the holy things that the Israelites were to bring to the Lord (22 :1–9). When the priest had any ritual uncleanness, he was not to approach or handle any of the gifts brought by the people and so defile the sanctuary (v. 3). To do such a despicable thing would mean being cut off by the Lord, a just penalty. Here we see again the type of the perfect Messiah High Priest, a fulfillment nothing can destroy. The servant of the Lord today needs also to examine his own heart attitude and to check any tendency that would render him unclean, thereby ruining his ministry.

Furthermore, every care was taken concerning the use of the holy gifts for food (vv. 4–7). Of the prescribed sacrifices, a priest could eat nothing from them if he 1) had a skin disease or a bodily discharge, 2) touched a thing or person who had touched a corpse, 3) had a seminal emission, 4) touched any unclean crawling thing to make him unclean, or 5) touched any unclean person for any reason. If any of these conditions occurred, he had to go through the prescribed ritual for cleansing before eating the holy food. A priest did not eat meat from any carcass found dead or torn by other beasts, prescriptions mentioned already for the ordinary person but repeated here because of the sacredness of the priest's office. He must be seen in the Law as the forerunner of the coming Messiah High Priest. The penalty was severe if a priest chose to disregard these laws to gratify his fleshly appetite; death was the penalty for defiling the special, priestly charge of the Lord (v. 9). The minister of Christ is also to be separated before the Lord and sensitive to the Lord's commands for satisfactory service.

Further safeguards were indicated for the food of the sanctuary (vv. 10–16). No one who was not a priest was to eat of the holy things of the sanctuary. This excluded the alien or a hired worker who was living temporarily with a priest (v. 10). Only those of the priest's household were able to eat of the sanctuary food, including slaves attached to the household. If a priest's daughter married a non-priest, she was not able to eat of her father's food any longer since she was part of another household (v. 12); however, if this woman became a widow or was divorced and there had been no children, she could return to her father's house and eat once more the holy food (v. 13). If a nonpriest ate of the holy food unintentionally, he had to repay the priest the offering, including restitution of one-fifth of the value of the gift offered (v. 14; Lev. 5). This penalty taught the offender that he had defrauded God and so had to make good. The priests were also warned concerning sharing their food with nonpriests (vv. 15–16). Even though the offer to share was well meant, to do so constituted sin for both priest and people. The religious leaders actually contributed to the rise or fall of the people and had to be careful. This principle never changes, even in our day. If the pulpits are strong and ministers' lives are godly, they influence communities to live on a high, moral plane. Otherwise, communities and nations head downward.

B. Laws Pertaining to Different Aspects of the Sacrifices (22:17–33)

The Israelites were reminded again about the kinds of animals they were to offer to the Lord (vv. 17–25). No matter what the offering, each had to be perfect (vv. 20, 21), none could have any defects (vv. 20–24). The only exception was an animal presented as a freewill offering (v. 23). If anyone dared to offer animals with defects, it would show the grossest ungratefulness to the God who had blessed so abundantly. Long after the Babylonian dispersion, the people were asked if they would like to present their blind and sick animals as gifts to their civil authorities (Mal. 1:8). Of course, the people would not dare do this. Then why do otherwise with the Lord?

Of even greater significance was the type misrepresentation of the sacrifice when defective animals were used. The type was never to be tampered with so as to mislead a people in the appreciation of Messiah's ministry. While we live today in the age of the New Covenant, this does not mean that the sacrificial animals of the Old Covenant are of no concern to us. They enable us to see 1) the relationship between the identification with and the death of the animals and the work of the Messiah in His death, and 2) they remind us never to take a liberal approach to theology, which discounts the atonement through Christ's substitutionary death. Christ did not die as a martyr for a good cause or as an example of a supreme dedication. There is a divine tie between the sacrificial system of the Law and the death of Jesus Christ on the cross, and this tie can never be broken.

Opportunity was also given to foreigners and strangers to offer sacrifices to God. As already seen, one purpose of the Law was to attract the pagans of other nations and provide opportunity for them to become a part of the Commonwealth of Israel. When foreigners observed, understood, and accepted the implications of the Law in its moral setting and with its emphasis on salvation and dedication to the one and true God, they were allowed to join themselves to the people of Israel and then had full rights as Israelites. If a stranger desired to live among Israel and offer sacrifices, the Law gave him permission to do so (vv. 18–19), but he had to proceed in the prescribed manner of the Word (v. 25). Evangelism was very much alive in the days of the Old Testament because through the witness of Israel thousands of pagans learned about the one true God and came to know Him.

In the closing instructions of this chapter we see how the Law expressed a humaneness in the choice of animals for the sacrifices (vv. 26–28), e.g., no newborn animal was used until seven days had passed; no female and its newborn were to be offered on the same day. Compassion was the keynote so that the female did not suffer needlessly; nor were animals slaughtered heartlessly. Even the way they were killed was regulated to minimize suffering. But if we see a compassion for the animals to be killed, should we not also sense the feelings of the antitype, Jesus, who died for our sins? He is divine, but He is also the Son of Man, who knew what it was to feel deeply about every human experience, even to the very end, when He cried, "My

God, my God, why have you forsaken me?" (Matt. 27:46; see Ps. 22:1).
His suffering and agony can only humble us and touch our hearts.

Once again the Law reminded the worshiper not to leave any of
the flesh of the thanksgiving offering until the second day (vv. 29–30;
Lev. 7). Obedience was of primary importance for five reasons: 1) "I
am the LORD." God's authority stands behind the spoken word. 2) "I
must be acknowledged as holy by the Israelites." This was meant to
encourage a response to live out His word and be a testimony to the
uniqueness of Israel's God. 3) "I am the LORD, who makes you holy."
The emphasis here was on Israel as an elect nation, a nation distinctly
set apart to God. 4) "I am the LORD, who . . . brought you out of
Egypt, to be your God" (see Exod. 3:14). The Redeemer's work was
seen at first as a national deliverance, but broadened to include the
spiritual. 5) A final reason can be a paraphrase to sum up the intent of
verses 31–33: "I am your God, the one true God, and not a tribal deity
like one of the gods or goddesses of the pagans" (see Lev. 22:31–33). It
was a high privilege then (because of the five points above the Israelites
were called to obedience), to be responsible in their dedication. Having been bought with a price, we likewise honor, adore, and serve our
God so as to bring glory to His name.

For Further Study

1. In a Bible dictionary or encyclopedia (see bibliography) read
articles on: defile, divorce, first-born, foreigner, marriage, mourning.

2. In addition to the Scripture covered in this chapter, read Deuteronomy 22:13–29. While the certificate of divorce was provided (Deut.
24:1), generally for the unsaved among the household of Israel, were
there safeguards and examples to curb the divorce rate? Why is the situation different in the body of Christ (e.g., the composition of the body)?

3. It is charged sometimes that the law contains only do's and
don'ts and is not spiritual. Make a study of the New Testament for the
many injunctions which seek to prevent the defiling of believers today,
starting perhaps with the word "defile" in a concordance.

4. Prepare a list of reasons why people offered the worst of their
animals for sacrifice and kept back gifts and offerings which should have
been presented to God.

5. Can you name individuals and peoples of the nations who
heard and observed the witness of the people Israel and even came to
the Lord?

Chapter 8

Law of the Sacred Calendar
(Leviticus 23:1–44; 25:1–55)

Important also for worship were the appointed feasts and festivals when Israel as a congregation was to assemble before the Lord (23:1–2). Moses had already provided some basic instruction (Exod. 23:14ff.), but in Leviticus information as to the appointed times was expanded to define the basic calendar of worship. Events on the calendar will be treated consecutively (chs. 23 and 25), and in the next chapter of this commentary the duties of the priests will be described (ch. 24).

A. The Sabbath (23:3)

The Sabbath (23:3) was first mentioned in Genesis 2:2, when God rested from His work of creation involving times, seasons, and life on earth. In the Law, therefore, it was reiterated that because God had ceased from all His labors, man must do likewise after working for six days (Exod. 20:9–11). The seventh day was blessed of the Lord (Gen. 2:3), and man found that blessing in it for his physical and spiritual renewal.

On the Sabbath there was to be complete rest (physical) and holy convocation (spiritual refreshing) before the Lord. God never intended the Sabbath to become what developed in the traditional, oral law of Israel. In the days of Jesus we find a multitude of laws making rest such a heavy burden that the common people could hardly enjoy the refreshment God intended. This provoked Jesus' comment that the Sabbath was for man's benefit, and never the reverse (Mark 2:27). This writer is not contending for a loose interpretation of the Sabbath because there had to be a general understanding of what it meant to not do any work. It should not be forgotten, either, that the rest that God desired for man's benefit was also to include spiritual renewal in the Word of God, not merely to be lounging around without any responsibility to the God of Israel.

After the resurrection of Jesus on the first day of the week, we find the disciples breaking bread on that day and generally observing it as the day on which the Lord was raised from the dead. We must not assume that the disciples, who were Jewish, disregarded the seventh day. There is every evidence that for at least two centuries there were both Jewish believers and Gentile believers who observed two days, the seventh day as well as the first day. (However, we need to realize that for Jewish believers in Israel, the first day of the week was a work day, and so on the first day worship was an evening affair, either Saturday evening or Sunday evening.) When the church became predominately non-Jewish, the seventh day was dropped as a day of worship, and the first day of the week was officially adopted as being appropriate for rest and worship. The first day of the week has *not* taken over as the Sabbath Day of the church, because the New Testament nowhere refers to the first day of the week as the Sabbath Day but rather keeps the two days distinct and separate.

The Sabbath is also used as a picture of a peace that comes from the knowledge of sins forgiven. While Canaan provided physical rest after Israel's desert wandering, the salvation experience gave spiritual rest to the Old Testament believer. The ministry of Jesus made possible a Sabbath rest for the people of God (Heb. 4:10) by which the soul no longer suffers from guilt and the penalty of sin but has peace and enjoys genuine rest. Someday there will also be a millennial rest when the earth will be released from the chains of the curse placed upon it (Gen. 3:17; Rom. 8:20–22).

B. The Passover (v. 5 [March–April])

Since Israel was an agricultural community in her origin, calendar observances were connected with the cycle of the harvesting of crops. The first feast on the religious calendar was the Passover, which was a memorial of Israel's release from bondage in Egypt. The feast took place in the evening on the fourteenth day in the first month, the month Nisan. The celebration of the deliverance event centered in a meal called the *seder*, referring to an order of service. Jewish people have gradually embellished the ceremony across the years of the Old

Testament, during the New Testament period, and ever since. The Gospels briefly refer to a simple order of service, the one followed by Jesus and His disciples just before His crucifixion as they, too, observed a Passover meal, or *seder*, which came to be known as the Last Supper.

The word "Passover" (v. 5; Exod. 12:1ff.) described the occasion when the angel of the Lord crossed over Egypt and spared the first-born in homes marked by the blood of a lamb on the doorposts. If they were not marked, the angel slew the first-born children in that home, and even the first-born of the cattle (Exod. 12:29). Only this severe measure finally persuaded the pharaoh of the Exodus to let Israel leave Egypt.

All Israel knew that the Passover commemorated a deliverance from physical bondage. However, the Lord also intended that through that deliverance and the subsequent revelation at Mt. Sinai the nation should learn the meaning of spiritual redemption. As God was sensitive to the cry of the physically afflicted, so He was also sensitive to those in spiritual bondage. Just as the Israelites were to be free from slavery to their Egyptian taskmasters, so the people of God were to be free from the chains of sin and were to be able to live in the Spirit as God desired. The term "Lord's Passover" was used to describe not only the shedding of blood to release the Israelites from Egypt but also thereafter to refer to the shedding of blood as a necessity to release them from the penalty of sin as indicated in the Levitical system.

The New Testament builds on this concept; thus, Paul declared that "Christ our Passover lamb, has been sacrificed" (1 Cor. 5:7) for us. It is in the light of these words that we see the meaning of the name Jesus (Heb. *Yehoshua*): "He will save his people from their sins" (Matt. 1:21). There is rich meaning in John the Baptist's declaration that the Lamb of God takes away the sin of the world (John 1:29), since he regarded Jesus as the Passover Lamb. In the *seder* at which Jesus sat with His disciples (now called the Last Supper), He took the third cup at the end of the meal, the cup of redemption, and instituted the cup of the Lord's table to picture the shedding of His blood for salvation. Redemption means identification with Jesus as the Passover Lamb.

C. The Feast of Unleavened Bread (vv. 6–8 [March–April])

Closely associated with the Passover was the Feast of Unleavened Bread. The Passover occurred on the fourteenth day of the first month, and the succeeding feast began on the fifteenth. This day was regarded as a Sabbath and no work except preparation of food was to be done. There was also a convocation of the people before the Lord. We do not know the details of the ancient observance of this feast, but perhaps we can see that as the fourteenth day was a remembrance of the meaning of the Passover, carefully worked out in the *seder*, so the one-week feast was a reminder of the eating of unleavened bread when the people hurriedly left Egypt. The Passover commemorated the shedding of blood as the final step in Israel's redemption, while the need to eat bread with no leaven showed the *consequence* of their deliverance (Exod. 12:39). These worship occasions are reminders to us to meditate with gratitude upon our salvation and not be flippant about it. The last day of this feast was also a day of rest and an occasion for a convocation and the days in between some light work was permitted.

While the Old Testament clearly divides the two worship occasions, Passover and the Feast of Unleavened Bread, by the time we come to the period of the New Testament, these two feasts were merged into one. In Matthew 26:17 and Mark 14:12 we note that the Passover is called the first day of unleavened bread, and therefore on the evening of the Passover the Feast of Unleavened Bread began.

D. The Sheaf of Firstfruits (vv. 9–14)

The ceremony of the offer of the sheaf of firstfruits was connected with the Feast of Unleavened Bread and took on full significance once the people were in the land and able to give offerings from their crops.

The offer of the sheaf relates the feast to an agricultural harvest. This was the time of year for the barley harvest in the land of Israel, and the sheaf offered to the Lord represented the whole harvest. It was to be waved before the Lord on the day *after* the first day of the Feast of Unleavened Bread (v. 11), which was a day regarded as a Sabbath. The sheaf was brought to a priest, who waved it before the Lord, i.e., before the altar of burnt offering (v. 11). At the same time the priest offered a male lamb for a burnt offering (v. 12). In preparing for the sheaf offering, designated persons were to go out in the fields to gather a representative sheaf during the evening of the fifteenth of Nisan. Then on the sixteenth day the priest waved the sheaf. Therefore, at the time the nation symbolically asserted its dedication in the national burnt offering (Exod. 29:38–42), it also affirmed its gratitude for the harvest of barley that was to follow. To insure acceptance of the sheaf offering and the harvest itself, no one was to eat any bread, roasted grain, etc., of that harvest (v. 14) until the offering of the sheaf. It was as if the whole harvest was gratefully presented to the Lord and that in return God gave it back to His people for their physical sustenance.

With the sheaf and burnt offerings there was also a meal offering of double the amount associated with the national burnt offering; this meal offering honored God for a bountiful harvest. A libation of wine was also given to signify the joyous occasion (v. 13).

Interestingly enough, the first time a sheaf was waved before the Lord was probably just after Israel entered the land of Canaan, having crossed the Jordan. On the fourteenth day of the first month the household of Israel observed the Passover on the desert plains of Jericho (Josh. 5:10–12), and on the following day they ate of the produce of the land, unleavened cakes and parched grain; they no doubt had cut a sheaf of the first fruits of the land to wave before the Lord. Significantly, the day after the people had eaten of the produce of the land, the manna ceased, and from then on the Israelites ate the food of the land.

The New Testament builds upon this established worship procedure when Paul indicates that Christ is the firstfruits and that after His resurrection there will be a resurrection for those who are His at His coming (1 Cor. 15:20, 23). Christ's ministry shows a blessed design in being linked to the sequence of the Old Testament feasts. The Lord's Passover is related to His death, and in His resurrection He is the firstfruits of those who are asleep (1 Cor. 15:20), strongly implying there will be a large harvest. Israel could know salvation in the emphasis of the ancient Passover since, while they ate of the barley harvest, they were reminded of deliverance from the empty, arid wilderness and simultaneously of spiritual deliverance. The first-century believer came to know the Lord in much the same way, as he believed in Jesus as the Passover Lamb.

E. Feast of Weeks (vv. 15–22 [May–June])

The Old Testament Feast of Weeks is the New Testament Pentecost. It receives its name from the way that the date for the feast was established. The people were to count from the day after the Sabbath, which was the day the sheaf of barley was presented, the sixteenth day of Nisan, or of the first month. Seven Sabbaths, or seven weeks, were counted, and then they were to add one day, making it fifty days after the offering of the sheaf of the firstfruits of the barley (vv. 14–25). This holy day came in the third month of the religious calendar year. The day was fixed and was actually observed for two days to insure an accurate calculation for the offering of the firstfruits of the wheat harvest.

The firstfruits of the wheat harvest were not presented as a sheaf but rather with enough grain (double the usual meal offering), along with leaven, to bake two loaves of bread (v. 17). The offering of these loaves became a special occasion, requiring the presence of all the male members of the nation (Exod. 23:14–17).

To prepare for this occasion, the officiating priest presented a male goat as a sin offering for the nation (Lev. 23:19), followed by burnt offerings for the nation and the officiating priest (v. 18), and then meal offerings. Central in this event was the offering of the firstfruits of the wheat harvest (v. 20) as it was waved before the altar of burnt offering (v. 21). It could not be presented *on* the altar because of the presence of leaven, or yeast, in the bread. The offering of the harvest to God (symbolized by the waving of the loaves) and its return to the people from the Lord reiterates what has already been discussed in the offering of the barley harvest.

The leaven in the bread seems to have pictured a people who were not all purified from their sins. While Israel was an elect nation, many of her individuals still had not entered into a redemption experience, necessitating the round of Levitical offerings before a priest could wave the loaves of firstfruits. Consequently, here was another reminder that the unredeemed within the nation should respond to the gracious offer of salvation of the Lord. No wonder Paul declared that the Law was a schoolmaster to lead one to the Messiah (Gal. 3:24); such tutoring began in the days of the Old Testament through the glorious presentation of rich, spiritual truths from the various sacrifices. The peace offerings associated with the firstfruits of the wheat harvest came last (v. 19), climaxing the whole gamut of worship experience of the Levitical offerings.

We repeat that in the New Testament, in following the calendar sequence of the Old Testament, the divinely inspired writers described the firstfruits in the body of Christ. It is significant that Jesus told His disciples in His postresurrection ministry that they were to wait for the promise of the Father and not to leave Jerusalem for any premature ministry (Acts 1:4). They were to bide their time until the Day of the Firstfruits, or Pentecost. In blessed design, just as the loaves of bread offered on this day signified the presence of the entire wheat harvest, so the salvation of the 3,000 on that particular day pledged the presence of all of Christ's own in His body. The yeast in the loaves of bread signified that the 3,000 and the rest who would follow, though free from the penalty of sin, were still not delivered from the presence of sin. It should be apparent that the church today should not ignore its legacy in the Old Testament round of worship.

The Feast of Weeks was an occasion for a holy convocation (v. 21). Minimum work was permitted, but opportunity was given for attending the offering of the loaves of the firstfruits. For this reason, on the occasion of the birthday of the church many people in and around Jerusalem, along with visitors from abroad, were present for temple worship in the early part of the day on Pentecost. This gave a maximum number of people an opportunity to hear the message of Peter when he preached, filled with the Holy Spirit.

The Lord repeated His warning concerning reaping corners of the barley and wheat fields (Lev. 23:22; 19:9). As already discussed, those who had an abundance were reminded to share with the needy. On Pentecost those who enjoyed blessings in abundance were to subsequently share their spiritual faith. We are reminded to give of our physical and spiritual blessings to those who do not have them.

F. Important Days of the Seventh Month (vv. 23–24)

The seventh month of the religious calendar (the first month of the civil calendar) was extremely important in the worship experience of the nation because the number seven emphasized a perfection and a peak in the worship that pertained to every person in the household of Israel.

A day of special trumpet blowing (vv. 23–25 [September–October])

After the Babylonian exile this day of special trumpet blowing, the Feast of Trumpets, was also celebrated as the New Year (Rosh Hashanah) because of its connection with the civil year calendar. On the first day of every month trumpets were blown over the burnt and peace offerings (Num. 10:10); but the first day of the seventh month was a special occasion for trumpet blowing, a reminder of the coming Day of Atonement on the tenth day. While the first day of the month had its appointed number of animals for various offerings (Num. 28:11–15), the first day of the seventh month saw an increase in the

number (Lev. 23:25; Num. 29:2-6), a further emphasis on the importance of the season (v. 24). This day was like a Sabbath and opportunity
was given for the people to have a holy convocation as the special
offerings were presented to the Lord (v. 25).

In time the days between the first and the tenth of the month
came to be known as solemn days, and Jewish people still refer to the
"Days of Awe," a time of preparation for the Day of Atonement, when
Israel was to consider the sin question. The unredeemed, especially,
were to reflect on their life styles and to repent of wrongdoing.

Once again we see in the calendar its prophetic implications. Paul
describes the occasion when Jesus will reappear to take away the
church, His body; there will be a shout, the voice of an archangel, and
the trumpet call of God (1 Thess. 4:16). Joel described the blowing of
the trumpet of alarm prior to the Day of the Lord and the time of
Jacob's trouble (Joel 2:1ff.), and this relates to the meaning of the
trumpet sound for Israel at the time of the Rapture of the body of
Christ, since the Rapture will come in the midst of the ingathering of
Israel from their dispersion. But the trumpet call in the Rapture will be
the signal to remind Israel to prepare for repentance.

The Day of Atonement (vv. 26–32 [September–October])

On the tenth day of the seventh month, beginning on the evening
of the ninth day and from that evening to the next evening, Israel had
its solemn Day of Atonement (Lev. 16). It was a day on which no work
was to be done, and if anyone attempted it, God would judge severely
(vv. 28, 30–31). This prohibition was given three times so that
everyone would understand the solemnity of the occasion.

In addition, we notice that the humbling, or affliction of the soul
mentioned three times (vv. 27, 29, 32), which is understood as fasting
and even putting on sackcloth and sitting in ashes (Isa. 58:3, 5). However, sorrow in itself does not take away sin; in fact, the sorrow of the
world produces death (2 Cor. 7:10), and this is precisely what God
wanted Israel to avoid. There is an affliction of the spirit that takes away
the desire for sin, and it was God's desire that on this day, the Day of
Atonement, when Israel was cleansed positionally, individuals com-
prising the nation would also find personal cleansing from sin and the
assurance of God's acceptance of them.

Once again, remembering that the trumpet call for the church in
her Rapture will also be a call to repentance to unbelieving Israel, we

should observe the unique, prophetic import of the Day of Atonement. There will be the time of Jacob's trouble just prior to the coming of the Messiah to *earth*, when the very soul of Israel will be afflicted in a holocaust of unprecedented proportions (Zech. 13:8–9). But just as there was the possibility of the assurance of the forgiveness of sin at the end of the Day of Atonement, so the day will come on the prophetic calendar when the whole remnant of Israel will be redeemed (Zech. 12:10).

The Feasts of Booths (vv. 33–44 [October])

The fifteenth day of this seventh month was the occasion of the Feast of Booths, lasting seven days (vv. 24, 39). The full description of the feast is not given here (see Num. 29:12–38), but its occurrence is mentioned in this Levitical passage in two different descriptions (vv. 33–36; 39–43). The first one merely announces the fact that Israel is to celebrate the Feast of Booths, while the second provides some details for its observance.

This feast marked the final ingathering of the crops in the fall of the year (v. 38; Exod. 23:16), and the people had reason to rejoice before the Lord because of the blessings meant for their well-being. Seven days were provided for this expression; and the first and eighth days were special, because on them the people were not to do regular work (vv. 36, 39). Opportunity was given for attendance at convocations and for participation in the offerings.

During the week the people were to live in booths, which were made of palm branches, boughs of leafy trees, and willows of the brook, large enough for a family to sit under and take their meals. The booths were decorated with the products and fruits of the land, a reminder of the Lord's blessings. As the family spent time in these temporary dwellings, they reflected on their past experiences, or those of their ancestors, of living in booths when wandering in the dry and arid desert (v. 43), and they were thankful for dwelling in a land flowing with milk and honey (v. 40). In view of this contrast of reflections and in view of their affliction of soul experienced on the Day of Atonement already past, was there not cause for rejoicing and great joy? To have the feast was a perpetual statute for Israel's native-born (v. 42).

By the first century Jewish people had further developed the occasion of this feast. The seventh day became quite a festive experience; there was a procession to the pool of Siloam to get water in a golden pitcher. This was brought back to the temple area and poured out at the altar amidst a display of joy in singing and dancing. This background gives meaning to Jesus' words when He took part in the celebration: "If a man is thirsty, let him come to me and drink" (John 7:37). His plea to the people gathered in honor of the sacred season was that they remember the One pictured in the rich symbolism; He would be more than adequate to give rivers of satisfying, living water within their inner beings (John 7:38).

The eighth day was also a day of convocation as we have already seen above. It was a special day; it was an assembly (Lev. 23:36), "a day of restraint" or "closing up." The eighth day was the close of the festivals of the whole year. The Israelites who had come to Jerusalem (either for the week or at the beginning of the month), after partaking in the convocation before the Lord on this day, would begin to prepare for return to their homes, taking back joys and blessings to families and friends.

The Feast of Booths also has prophetic significance concerning Israel and the fullness of the kingdom. Following the restoration of the remnant of Israel, those unregenerate of the nations who turn to God will enter into the kingdom rest and enjoy the peace, joy, and blessings of a Feast of Booths on an international scale. Israel will celebrate the Feast of Booths again in the fullness of the kingdom, and representatives of all nations will be in attendance in Jerusalem, joining their hosts in honoring and worshiping the Lord, from whom all blessings flow (Zech. 14:16).

Moses concludes the chapter by making a summarizing statement about the yearly festivals (Lev. 23:44). Does all this seem tedious to believers today? Some may declare that we are no longer under the Law and that we are to have freedom in worship. While avoiding ritualistic observance, people need appointed times and regularity in worship. Even secular pursuits require discipline and dogged determination. And how can we begin to know the Lord and grow in Him unless we lay hold diligently, in a methodical manner, on all that He has for us?

G. The Sabbatical Year (25:1–7)

As soon as the Israelites entered the land, they were to observe stated occasions over long periods of time, and therefore they began to count the years so as to observe a seventh year of rest as a Sabbath to the Lord. The people were to sow their fields for six years, and for six years they were to prune and gather from the vineyards (v. 3; Exod. 23:10). For six years the people were to labor in tilling the soil, but on the seventh year the land was to have a Sabbath rest to the Lord (v. 4; Exod. 23:11). The harvest's aftergrowth was not to be reaped, and neither were the grapes of unpruned vines to be gathered (Lev. 25:5). The only ones who could take from the fields in this year were the needy; whatever was left over, the beasts of the field could eat (Exod. 23:11). To skeptics, who wondered how they would manage until the end of the eighth year, the Lord said that they could eat what grew of itself in the seventh year and that the sixth year's harvest would be great enough to last until the next official one (vv. 6, 7, 21). No farmer's skill would make the land produce the extra amount; nor would superabundance come by transgressing the Law altogether and working the land in the seventh year.

Think of the situation described here. The people were to have peace and quiet and opportunity to enjoy leisure for the Lord's service as well as to have time for themselves. What a grand testimony to neighboring peoples and countries! Would they not inquire as to why people were not working? Through this experience God intended to draw many into the Commonwealth of Israel, or at least to provide a witness to the certainty of knowing the Lord.

In the sabbatical year the land also rested. Six years of crops and vineyards take a great deal out of the soil. We know today from scientific farming that it is necessary to let farmland rest and to replace nutrients in the soil taken out by growing plants. In the Mosaic Covenant God wisely provided for needs now recognized in modern agriculture.

The Chronicler indicated that the Babylonian Exile took place because it was necessary for the land to enjoy its Sabbaths (2 Chron. 36:21), since few in the preexilic period had made any attempt to keep the sabbatical year. For what reasons? Little faith? Greediness? Apathy in spiritual matters? While there is no equivalent for a universal sabbatical today, basic human attitudes to the clear commands of God do not change; either we respond to His Word for our blessing and rest in our souls, or we turn against His Word, a rebellion leading ultimately to our hurt.

The sabbatical year also called for a remission of debts (Deut. 15:1–3). With every succeeding sabbatical year all creditors had to release debtors in Israel; ungodly pagans outside the Covenant's influence still had to pay their debts, however. Still, no creditor among the people of God had the right to oppress another person. Seven years was the statute of limitations for owing debts, and in the year when the land had its rest, God's word also granted peace of mind and rest to one burdened with a debt he was unable to repay. This is one law carried over to our Western society—to mark the limit when all debts must be dropped by creditors.

The sabbatical year has also been seen by some as having prophetic import. As the seventh day was considered a day of rest and as the seventh month of the religious calendar marked a cessation within the farming year, so the seventh year will mark a rest of a thousand years after six thousand years of woe. Some have therefore seen the earth passing through six "world" days of one thousand years each and have regarded the seventh "day" as a time of joy, rest, and peace on the earth.

H. The Year of Jubilee (25:8–55)

Regulations governing the Year of Jubilee comprise a piece of legislation unique in all the literature of the ancient Middle East. In these provisions one sees again the wisdom of God in the political, economic, and social affairs of a people holy to Him.

Provisions and instructions (vv. 8–22)

In the forty-ninth year from the previous year of Jubilee, which would be a sabbatical year, the ram's horn was sounded on the Day of Atonement to announce the beginning of a new Jubilee. It lasted for one year, marking the fiftieth year as a significant period. The two consecutive years constituted a special time of blessing—the sabbatical and then the Jubilee. Most people and families could share in this special occasion at least once in a lifetime.

There was first a glad proclamation of release. Each one returned to his allotted property and to his own family (vv. 10, 13). In the normal course of life misfortunes came, and people and families had to sell their land or enter into servitude to cover debts, etc. But when the Year of Jubilee came around, all land reverted to its original owners. The chief point was that there should never be a build-up of power by a few to control the land and the people; therefore, there was a redistribution of the land as it had been divided in the beginning. We need to recognize the wisdom and beneficence of God who gave people and families opportunity for new beginnings, in spite of what monied people might call this state of affairs.

This should not be seen merely as a wild, share-the-wealth plan. Rather, each family had an opportunity to work their own land again and to create their own wealth. Furthermore, land itself belonged to the Lord, and Israel really lived on the land as trustees. Therefore, no one was to sell farmland for all time as if it belonged to him (v. 23). Land could be sold only on the basis of the value of crops until the next Year of Jubilee (vv. 14–17), keeping in mind that this did not include the sabbatical years. In no way should a brother Israelite do wrong or defraud another. The Law in this instance puts its finger on possible selfishness and warns against it, for it would be an affront against the real Landowner (v. 17). For this reason King Ahab himself did not force Naboth in the matter of his land. It took a pagan, Jezebel, to force the issue (1 Kings 21). What did this pagan care about the Word of God? God, as the Landowner, took notice however and had His vindication.

In the Year of Jubilee the land was not to be tilled either, and so for two consecutive years the people were released from their toil; the same instructions as to the use of the land for the sabbatical also applied to the Jubilee year (vv. 11–12). For those who were really skeptical, God's reply was that He would so order His blessing in the sixth year that there would be enough food for three years (vv. 20–21). Here we see two diametrically opposed forces that are always in operation: trust and unbelief in the God-and-man relationship. God had taken care of Israel from their time in Egypt to their entering Canaan; and now, would He not also provide enough in the sixth year to last until the harvest at the end of the ninth year (v. 22)? Likewise, cannot God do for us far beyond what we can ask or think?

As a final warning people were encouraged to observe the statutes and judgments of God so that they could live securely and so that the land might produce abundantly (vv. 18–19).

The redemption of inheritances (vv. 23–34)

We have noted that land sales were, in reality, based on crop values until the next Year of Jubilee. But the sales values agreed upon also became the redemptive values. The Law recognized that inequities are common, but there was always the attempt to minimize financial misfortunes. Suppose someone, because of reverses, needed money (v. 25) and therefore had to sell his land? This state of affairs was to be as temporary as possible. As soon as convenient the nearest kinsman was to buy back the land, based on its crop value for only the length of time the purchaser had held it. The unfortunate person was given the opportunity to as quickly as possible become financially solvent so that he could pay back his near kinsman. If an unfortunate person did not have someone to redeem him, he himself had the right to redeem his own land, if possible, again based on crop value for as long as the purchaser had held it (vv. 26–27). But if the poor fellow could not repurchase the land and had no near kinsman to do this for him, he and his family had to wait until the Year of Jubilee before he could get possession of the land without payment. In addition, because of the call for kinsmen to redeem lost property on behalf of unfortunate relatives, there was also the attempt to preserve family ties in places of origin. The idea was to prevent dispersion of families, thereby destroying the unity of family genealogies. Among the people of God, families were their brothers' keepers and were not to see them become wards of an indifferent community.

Having noted these beneficial laws, we can now appreciate the circumstances of Naomi and Ruth and can see the way in which Boaz acted as the kinsman-redeemer. We can also appreciate the promise that the Redeemer will one day come to Zion to redeem Israel, preparing them for the messianic kingdom (Isa. 59:20; Rom 11:26). In individual salvation Jesus Christ became our Kinsman-Redeemer when He took upon Himself flesh and blood (Heb. 2:14); and although He does not force His desires upon us, He has the right and the power to redeem us from the bondage of sin. In this way many peoples from every nation, tribe, kindred, and tongue will find themselves released from their poor and lost position and able to be a part of the family of God. Christ also has the right someday to redeem the earth from its curse so that in the messianic kingdom there will be unparalleled blessings.

Redemption rights were limited regarding houses within the walls of a city. Upon the sale of a house the right of redemption was good for only one year, and if a house was not reclaimed, it passed in perpetuity to the purchaser and was not returned in the Year of Jubilee (vv. 29–30). Buildings outside the cities, situated on farmland, were considered part of the land, and their redemption rights were the same as those for the land itself (v. 31). A higher premium was placed on land than on houses because a living could be made from it, while houses could decay, burn, or rot out.

The Levites' houses were protected in every way (vv. 32–34). Their houses and the pasture lands of their cities could never be removed from them. One needs to recall that because of the curse on their father, Levi (Gen. 49:5–7), they could never own land as a tribe. They did redeem themselves in the camp at Sinai (Exod. 32:26ff.) and afterwards were made ministers of the Lord. The land for the Levitical cities was given to them by other tribes. Because of poverty a priest might have to sell his house, but it reverted to him in the Jubilee if it was not redeemed before that time. The pasture fields of the Levitical cities could not be sold, for these fields were the perpetual possession of the Levites. The main reason for all this protection was that all a Levite had was regarded as a gift from God.

Protection of the poverty-stricken (vv. 35–46)

Something needs to be said about the care of an Israelite who becomes very poor. This needy person was to be sustained by his countrymen or by members of his own tribe until he could help himself (v. 35). In this period money was not to be lent him at interest, and absolutely no interest was to be taken for food (vv. 35, 37). Those able to help were to remember that once they had been slaves in Egypt with no expectation of help except from the Lord, who later delivered them (v. 38). How then could they mistreat their needy brother and act like a pharaoh? Neither were they to look down on their unfortunate brother, but rather they were to revere God; to take advantage of the needy was equivalent to despising the Lord (v. 36). Can believers today do less than what was commanded then?

If the needy person had no prospect of ever repaying his debt, he had to sell himself to—perhaps to a creditor (2 Kings 4:1) or to another well-to-do person (v. 39). This was drastic action, but even in a case like this the Israelite owner could only treat the needy one as a hired person and could keep him only until the Jubilee ahead (v. 40). This did not apply to private debts, which were canceled during each sabbatical year (Deut. 15:1ff.), but rather to extreme poverty, in which, even after selling his land, a man still had desperate needs. The owner in this situation could not maltreat his brother Israelite or rob him of his dignity (Lev. 25:40, 43). He was doing God's bidding in caring for the needy as a hired servant. The Lord was their Advocate, saying that even the needy were His "servants" (v. 42) who also had been released from Egypt. A good example of extreme conditions in this regard appears in Scripture when Nehemiah severely reprimanded landowners in accordance with the Law (Neh. 5:1ff.); they had to acknowledge their wrongoing in oppressing the poor and had to rectify it.

Under the Law Israelites could buy slaves from the pagan nations or from the sons of the temporary residents living among you and members of their clans born in your country (Lev. 25:44–45) because the cultures of that day recognized slavery as a socially accepted practice. The Law did promise that if Israel was obedient to the word, she would experience material blessings without measure; slaves brought into this kind of economy would also share in it. And there was another consideration. If the slave would repudiate his idolatrous background and adopt the beliefs of the Israelites, he entered through conversion into the Commonwealth of Israel. From then on, he was considered an Israelite, and the Law applied to him. The Law did not abruptly overturn a socially established practice, but if Israelites respected it, it contained within itself a structure that would give eventual freedom to slaves. An element of this is seen in Paul's assessment of the slavery question in his day (Eph. 6:5–9). He did not insist on the immediate cessation of this social practice, but the attitude he required in the master-slave relationship in the Lord called for the freedom of the slave, and ultimately abolition of the practice itself. At the very least, the slave could attain the status of a hired servant with every human right.

Israelite hired to a non-Israelite (vv. 47–55)

There were cases in which, having sold his land, a needy Israelite then sold himself to a non-Israelite (v. 47), either an alien or temporary resident. In these cases the Israelite's claim upon Israel, or Israel's claim upon him, did not cease. Someone in his family, near or distant kin, could claim him and pay the purchase price. Or if the needy person came into means while in the service of an alien or temporary resident, the Israelite then had the right to redeem himself (vv. 48–49), his price to be based on a proportion of the agreed price for serving to the next Year of Jubilee (vv. 50–52). The Israelite refunded the portion of the price for which he did not serve. No unfair advantage was to be taken by either party. While the Israelite was serving, even though the temporary resident or alien was not an Israelite, the Law applied to the care of the needy Israelite. His status was that of a hired servant, and he was not to be mistreated. If there were no means for redemption, then the Law declared that the Israelite was freed from his bondage in the Jubilee and that he and his family could return to their land (v. 54). While difficult days are a part of life, the Jubilee always gave bright hope for the future, no matter what the current circumstances happened to be.

Just as the sabbatical year has prophetic import for the messianic kingdom, so the Jubilee also presages many aspects of the kingdom as well. The very word Jubilee seems to be derived from a word meaning "to restore" or "bring back." In relating this message to the kingdom, we note that this earth will be released from the bondage of sin and will again flourish as in the Garden of Eden. Israel and the peoples on the earth will experience a redemption from all the bitter consequences of sin. It will be truly a world at rest when the year of the "Redeemed" will come, when the Kinsman-Redeemer will sit on David's throne, and when the countries of the earth will live in peace.

For Further Study

1. In a Bible dictionary or encyclopedia (see bibliography) read articles on: convocation, fast, festivals (calendar), firstfruits, inheritance, jubilee, Passover, Pentecost, slave (service).

2. Has the Sabbath Day ever been revoked? Can you list some reasons why it has not been officially set aside?

3. Show how the offer of the sheaf of the first fruits of the barley and the first fruits of the wheat relate to significant New Testament truths.

4. Make a list of the prophetic significance of Rosh Hashanah, the Day of Atonement, and Feast of Booths.

5. Do you think the concept of jubilee can be applied today concerning ownership of land?

6. Starting with Leviticus 25 and extending to the rest of the Old Testament, show how the Law had much to say about the care of the poor and disadvantaged.

Chapter 9

Laws of Ritual and Equity of the Law
(Leviticus 24:1–33)

This chapter discusses some of the priests' duties and the basis upon which the judges were to execute the Law (Lev. 24:1–33).

A. The Golden Candlestick (vv. 1–4)

All the details for the construction of the golden candlestick base and shaft with its seven branches of pure gold is given in Exodus 25:31–39. This candlestick was to be placed in the Holy Place of the tabernacle, outside the veil, or curtain of testimony (Lev. 24:3). While the priests carried out their ministry in the light of the golden candlestick, the people also identified with the priests in their ministry to God since the sons of Israel, each in turn, brought the clear oil from beaten olives for the lamp stand. All the sons of Israel could sense that the message of the candlestick was to the whole nation.

The priests, serving by turn, every evening and every morning checked to see that the lamps were full, the wicks were trimmed, and the lights were continually burning (vv. 2–4). The lights were never allowed to go completely out, although some of the lamps either burned low or dimly. We must remember that this was the only means of light in the Holy Place, aside from the light of the presence of God in the Holy of Holies, in the tabernacle, and later in the Solomonic temple.

The lessons found here are significant. The golden candlestick, like all other furniture placed in the area next to the Holy of Holies, reminded one of intense dedication and cost in its construction. Giving toward and presenting such a costly article to the tabernacle was an expression of love and devotion on the part of the people. The seven branches of the candlestick symbolized perfection of the light of God among His covenant people. The sons of Israel were reminded of this light many times throughout their lives. Indeed, they had the light that came from revelation. David declared that the Lord was his light (Ps. 27:1) and that by the light of God Israel would be able to see (Ps. 36:9). The Word of God was to be the light for the way in which Israel should walk (Ps. 119:105), i.e., to know Him and to live godly before Him. To walk by any other light can only lead into darkness, where men grope their way trying to see; and when men substitute darkness for the light of God, He can only condemn their attempts (Isa. 5:20).

So important is the aspect of the light in the midst of God's people that we see Jesus using this symbol to describe His own presence and ministry as the Light of the World, first for His people Israel and then for the whole world (John 8:12; Rom. 1:16). This was specifically proclaimed in the midst of a people that invalidated the word of God by substituting many of the traditions of men (Mark 7:13). The light of God is still spread abroad today amidst the darkness of the philosophies and ideologies that lead mankind into further darkness. Jesus is the perfect light which, if men follow, will show the way to life. In this light we can be led out of our loneliness, confusion, and heartache into the bright rays of God's sunshine, by which we can know Him and live godly lives that will be an attraction to the world.

In another place in the New Testament we come across the symbolism of the candlestick, or lamp stands (Rev. 1:12–13; 20). John selected seven representative churches, whose spiritual conditions called either for the Lord's reproof or for His commendation (Rev. 1:20ff.). Note that there are seven candlesticks, each with their lamps, for the purpose of providing light, thereby emphasizing that the light of God is His revelation. The lamp stands symbolize the seven churches, among whom Christ walks; the symbolism is obviously a concept borrowed from the temple ministry in the midst of Israel. We see, then, that the churches were then and now to be as golden candlesticks, giving forth the light of God in the communities of the nations and providing opportunity for unbelievers and pagans to come to His light. Christ walks in the midst of these lights, indicating that He gave significance and meaning to these individual lights because He is the true and real light. May it ever be true of your congregation and mine—and may we heed the warning—that a lamp stand can be removed from its place because of apostasy and unbelief (Rev. 2:5).

B. The Bread of the Golden Table (vv 5–9)

The fashioning of the golden table associated with the bread is described in Exodus 25:23–30. It was situated in the Holy Place on the north side of the tabernacle (as the tabernacle faced the east) (Exod. 26:35). As in the case of the oil (Lev. 24:2), the sons of Israel, by turns, were to take fine flour, i.e, their best, and they were to bake twelve cakes with it using the prescribed amount (v. 5). Each cake contained twice the amount of the meal offering presented with the national burnt offerings (Num. 28:5) and was of a special significance when presented to the priests just before each Sabbath.

The officiating priest placed these cakes every Sabbath on the table designated for this purpose. The literal meaning of the Hebrew is "bread of the Presence" (in the older English versions it is rendered "shewbread"). The bread was arranged in two rows, six to a row (v. 6), as representative of the twelve tribes of Israel. On each row was placed a certain amount of incense (v. 7) as a memorial portion, indicating that the bread was accepted by the Lord. There it remained all week, and on the sixth day, before a new supply was received, the incense was burned to denote further that the bread had been accepted as an offering of fire; but at the same time the Lord returned the bread to the priests for their food (v. 9), to be eaten on the Sabbath in the court of the tabernacle.

The unique symbolism can be appreciated. The table of acacia wood overlaid with gold indicated the devotion and love of the people in their presentation of their gifts. The bread on the table, unleavened of course, is never to be seen in the light of a pagan concept of presenting food to some idol. Rather, this scene showed recognition that the God of Israel was ready to sustain His people beyond what they could ask or think. The twelve cakes, which were renewed every week, represented the tribes of Israel, and the double amount of flour in each cake over the regular offering at the altar, suggested that the Lord could provide superabundantly for every material need for every tribe. No matter what their curcumstances, all the sons of Israel had to do was to look to the central place of worship to be reminded of the bread cakes or the Presence bread, indication that the Lord knew of their needs.

The New Testament builds on this symbolism as well. Jesus the Messiah referred to Himself as the Bread of Life; those who partake of His life and teaching will never hunger or thirst (John 6:35), and consequently, neither can one have a part in the resurrection of the just without partaking of Him (John 6:54). The Presence bread is a symbol of one of the most precious truths associated with the sanctuary of God and is one of the most beautiful types in Scripture.

C. Penalty for Blasphemy and the Basis of Judgment (vv. 10–22)

A tragic fight between an Israelite and another man of a mixed marriage was described in this passage. The latter blasphemed the "name" (vv. 10–11), or the covenant name of the God of Israel, YHWH, rendered as "Lord." To this day Jewish people never utter this name but substitute instead Adonai, or the phrase used here, "the name," to underscore its sacredness. Upon hearing it, the people put the offender in custody until they had a word from God as to what his penalty should be (v. 12).

The sentence was death by stoning! Does this seem harsh? People today would say that such a God is cruel and heartless. But aren't penalties to be expected when we do wrong? In the physical world, if we do not follow the laws of hygiene and care for our bodies, don't we suffer penalties? If we decide to ignore the law of gravitation and to jump out the window, do we think we can float upward to suit our own fancies? And are there not also certain moral and spiritual laws which cannot be transgressed without appropriate penalties? One of these transgressions is to despise the Name that relates to the King of the universe. We cannot live in His world as His guests and still defy Him. To despise Jesus' name, which is above all names (Phil. 2:9), will also bring about a penalty—death.

Judgment for the blasphemer was to be applied impartially. If an alien despised the Name, he had to die. And even a blaspheming man whose mother must have been prominent among those in the tribe of Dan (v. 11) had to die. There were to be no favorites in the dispensing of justice.

The Law was impartial in all manner of offenses in man-to-man relationships. Many people stumble at the description of "eye for eye, tooth for tooth" (v. 20) and miss the important point of the impartial application of the Law, e.g., if one knocked out the tooth of another in a fight, the offender was not to be executed. Only in the case of murder was the penalty death, a sentence in force before the Law was given formally at Sinai (Gen. 9:6). Lesser injuries were to receive corresponding penalties. In the case of one's killing the beast of a neighbor, restitution was to be made. Equal justice was to apply to both Israelite and alien on an equitable basis, a legal concept generally accepted in the Judeo-Christian culture of the West.

D. Penalty for Blasphemy Carried Out (v. 23)

There was a quick execution of the blasphemer (v. 23). Witnesses testified that they had heard the offender (v. 14). The offender was then taken outside the camp, the witnesses laid their hands on his head, and the congregation stoned him to death (v. 14, 23). Tragic as these circumstances were, the penalties were designed to serve as a deterrent to other similar crimes. The people did not question the value of a deterrent; the laws were just, and the revelation of God was good. Not to apply but to question the value of the laws only served to flaunt the Lawgiver. Because we see fit today to despise God's basic laws, we suffer the consequences of lawlessness and the breakdown of order in society.

For Further Study

1. In a Bible dictionary or encyclopedia (see bibliography) read articles on: blasphemy, bread of Presence (tabernacle), candlestick (tabernacle), name of God.

2. List the understanding in the Old Testament and New Testament symbolism concerning the seven-branch golden candlestick.

3. The shewbread (bread of the Presence) was considered sacred. Why did the priest Ahimelech give this bread to David and his men as ordinary food to eat (1 Sam. 21:1–6)?

4. Do you feel you have the right to rebuke a nonbeliever when he uses God's name in vain?

5. Make a study of what is meant by the phrase "eye for eye, tooth for tooth."

Chapter 10

Law of Obedience
(Leviticus 26:1–46)

God promised rich temporal blessings upon Israel if she were obedient to His Word in its statutes, judgments, precepts, and laws. In conjunction with this chapter, one should also have Deuteronomy 28 before him for details that will provide further enlightenment.

A. Basis of Proper Worshp and Conduct (Lev. 26:1–2)

The first two commandments are emphatically stressed as constituting a guide for the sons of Israel. The points were plain: the Lord was to be first, and His people were to make no idols; they were to keep the Sabbaths holy and to appear before the Lord at the sanctuary at the appointed times. Failure in these areas is the root of spiritual and moral breakdown. The fall of a person or a nation comes because of a long series of sins that whittle away at the vitals of spiritual and moral strength. Sin and iniquity pile up, and sensitivities grow dull concerning the Word of God. It isn't long before people find themselves in the enemy's camp, but they don't quite realize what is wrong. Before Moses talked about his people's relation with their God and the attendant blessings or curses, he warned them to keep God's commandments before them as a guide for every detail of life.

B. Description of Blessings (vv. 3–13)

The distinction between the Abrahamic covenant and the Mosaic constitution is clear. The conditional aspect of the Mosaic covenant is seen again in the possibility of blessings for the sons of Israel: "If you follow my decrees and are careful to obey my commands, I will send you . . ." (vv. 3–4). The Abrahamic covenant established the relationship between the people of Israel and their God.

In rapid succession the Lord recited the conditional blessings. The Lord promised rains in their seasons, both the early and latter rains, so that the land would bear crops and the trees would bear their fruit in a dependable harvest (vv. 4–5). In fact, the Israelites would have to clear away the old to make way for abundant new harvests (v. 10). The land would enjoy peace, and no harmful beasts would be in the fields (v. 6). The divine promise was that no sword would be raised in the land and that if enemies dared to attack, He would enable the Israelites to chase their enemies in the fantastic proportions of five against a hundred and a hundred against ten thousand—and no enemy would ever prevail (vv. 6–8). The people themselves would be fruitful and multiply (v. 9). The presence of the Lord would remain in the midst of Israel in the sanctuary, and He would walk among them to acknowledge Israel as His peculiar people. Lest an Israelite imagine that he could accomplish all this by the arm of his own strength, he was reminded of his lowly background: the Israelites once had been slaves in the land of Egypt, and the only reason they were now free was because of God's direct intervention (v. 13).

C. The Warning (vv. 14–39)

In stark contrast to the description of blessings God warned of dire consequences if the sons of Israel did not obey Him but ignored His commands, rejected His decrees, and abhorred His laws. Not to listen to the Word of God was the equivalent of rejecting His rule, choosing rather to be guided by selfish ideas (vv. 14–15). There is danger in a lack of gratitude, and all believers need daily to take heed to guard their relationship with the Lord.

Six warnings followed, each more severe than the last. Sometimes God found discipline necessary to bring the people to their senses. In fact, a lack of needed discipline would seem to indicate a lack of concern on God's part.

First there was the warning of distress (vv. 16–17). People would live in dread and terror of their enemies. When the sons of Israel sowed their crops, their enemies would eat of the produce and harvest. The presence of God would be against the Israelites. The events of the Book of Judges are good illustrations of the results of not heeding this warning.

If the people should continue to be disobedient, the Lord warned, second, that He would bring drought upon the land (vv. 18–20) so as to correct their spiritual misdirection. He would break down their pride of power because pride, described as a "lifting up" in the Hebrew, is the greatest barrier that separates a person or people from God (Prov. 16:18). In order to bring about humility, the Lord would make the sky like iron and the earth like bronze, which would mean disaster in a land utterly dependent upon rain. Perhaps, with less food, the people would realize who the One is who makes the food supply possible, and they would return to the Lord.

The third warning was that of the terror of wild animals. Because of the increasing effects of the drought, wild and dangerous beasts would roam afar in search of food. So dangerously low would the food supply become that beasts would attack man, especially unsuspecting children, to satisfy hunger (vv. 21–22). The drastic measure in this warning was a desperate attempt to reach the hearts of the people when they would be bereaved.

If repentance still did not come after three warnings and resultant penalties because of continued sin, suffering would become more widespread. The fourth warning was that of the spread of disease (vv. 23–26). The sword of the Lord would strike against His people, subjecting them to plague. With continual heat and no rain cattle would begin to die, and even the trees would become subject to all kinds of disease. These are also the conditions that make for the spread of sickness in population centers. The rationing of food would leave the people so weak that they would become easy prey to their enemies. Further rebellion could only lead, fifth, to a frightful breakdown of moral decency (vv. 27–31). The famine would be so severe that people would become cannibals, a terrifying situation among a people who had been given God's revelation. Such scenes actually came to pass in Israel's history in times of great apostasy (2 Kings 6:26–30). The same kind of experience was repeated in the siege of Nebuchadnezzar against Jerusalem (Jer. 52:6; Lam. 4:10) and the very same circumstances occurred during the siege of Jerusalem by the Romans.

The most severe disciplinary warning of all, sixth, was dispersion (vv. 32–39). Enemies would take over the land of Israel and see nothing in it to make it desirable (v. 32). While the sons of Israel would be dispersed to wander aimlessly in foreign lands, the land was to rest and enjoy its Sabbaths (vv. 34–35). In the lands of dispersion Israel would roam afar to find rest to their souls, but they would never experience it apart from the land of Israel. The warnings prophesy such a fright among the dispersed people that even the sound of a wind-blown leaf would send them fleeing for safety when no one was chasing them. Death would come to many in the lands of their dispersion while they yearned desperately for a little peace of mind and soul. It is no wonder that when Israel was in Babylon, they could not sing the Lord's song in that foreign land (Ps. 137:4).

Some in Israel today will say that human effort has been responsible for the physical redemption of the land after 1900 years of dispersion. But the Lord alone can bring about a totality of physical and spiritual redemption for His people in the day of Jacob's trouble (Zech. 13:8–9) in the land of Israel so that they will finally acknowledge Him. These negative circumstances should *never* make the believer today boast with the pride Paul warned about in Romans 11:17–21. There is a positive design in all these circumstances directing God's people to return to Him, and we ought to be in tune with and sensitive to the will of God in these matters. The Babylonian exile preserved a remnant faithful to the Lord. Those who returned from Babylon were a godly remnant, who rebuilt the temple and restored worship. Those exiled from Israel in the first century and subsequent centuries also remind us of God's purposes. God in His mercy and grace made it possible for Jewish people who, although they did not recognize Jesus as Messiah in their land, did receive Him in the lands of their dispersion. God will prepare Israelis to recognize His truths and return to Him someday in the not too distant future.

In all the blessings and warnings the condition of the land was prominent. If the land was productive and bringing forth crops and fruit in abundance, it was an indication that the relationship with the Lord was right. If the conditions in the land were dismal, i.e., if there was drought, etc., it was a danger signal that called for repentance and return to the Lord. It is true that there is productivity today in the land of Israel, but this is only a temporary provision while God is bringing His people back home. One day yet to come Israel will shout for joy on the height of Zion and be radiant over the bounty of the Lord (Jer. 31:12).

D. The Preservation of a Remnant (vv. 40–46)

As already indicated, we see the wisdom of God in His disciplinary actions. The terms of the Abrahamic covenant preclude any disappearance of the sons of Israel from the pages of history (Gen. 17:7). If the people will confess their iniquity, if they will acknowledge their unfaithfulness before the God of Israel, and if they will humble their uncircumcised hearts (vv. 40–41), God will take note of the covenant He made with Jacob, Isaac, and Abraham and will "remember the land" (v. 42). The Abrahamic covenant is an unconditional covenant, which guarantees the perpetuity of the line of Jacob and allots the land of Israel to Jacob's descendants for as long as there is a history of the human race. The restoration to favor with God and the blessings upon the land are all intertwined with a good spiritual relationship between God and His people. Thus, when Daniel stood and confessed, representationally, his sins and the sins of his people, it was the signal for the deliverance of Daniel's people from their captivity and for their restoration to the land (Dan. 9:1–20). Someday this prayer will be repeated by Israel, and she will be delivered from all captivity and restored fully to her land (Zech. 13:9; 14:8–11).

For Further Study

1. In a Bible dictionary or encyclopedia (see bibliography) read articles on: blessing, dispersion (captivity), land, obedience, remnant.

2. Make a list of the progressive warnings by God to an unrepentant people.

3. What is the specific link between material blessings and spiritual well being? Why would the priests be so directly involved with one aspect of material blessings (or the lack of them)?

4. Has God promised to bless His people today with lavish material blessings if every spiritual dimension is right (see Phil. 4:19)?

5. Why do Jewish people remember their land, no matter where they have been dispersed, as they observe the main holidays?

6. Do you suppose the church, concerned in general with their outreach, has overlooked one main reason for the dispersion of Israel?

Chapter 11

Laws of Vows and Tithes
(Leviticus 27:1–34)

This chapter treats the dedication of persons and their possessions to God. No true worship can end without presenting ourselves and our substance to the Lord, Who provides all our benefits.

A. Dedication of Persons (vv. 1–8)

The meaning of making a singular, or special, vow has an extraordinary aspect to it. It might also have the idea, "to consecrate something vowed" (v. 2). A similar concept appears in Psalm 4:3, where the Lord says He has "set apart" the godly man. To consecrate a person in a vow was indeed an extraordinary move, and the rule was that he should be redeemed at a certain price, although in some cases the person was not redeemed, e.g., Samuel. A value was attached to such a consecrated person according to the valuation set by the congregation of Israel (v. 2), the valuation being the same for all persons within each rank, whether they were wealthy or poor (vv. 3ff.). If there was a very poor person, the priests made exception and arrived at an equitable valuation (v. 8).

The valuation was based upon the ranks of age and usefulness (vv. 3–8). Those in the prime of life are mentioned first, twenty to sixty years of age; the male was valued at fifty shekels of silver and the female at thirty. This was not meant to degrade the woman, but in the society of that day with its potentialities and actualities, values were measured accordingly. Values were likewise adjusted for the other ages within the two sexes.

One aspect of the vow was that it was never made in private. When one vowed himself or another person, e.g., a baby, it was to be done in public, and the community was to acknowledge the vow so as to prevent rash talk (Prov. 20:25). The vow then was visible, external declaration of the inner intent, secured by the payment of the valuation. A number of biblical contexts illustrate the vowing of persons as indicated in Lev. 27:2-8, either to belong to the Lord or to do His service: 1) In the dedication of the Nazarites when they were marked from birth, the vow was made by the parents, and the whole community became partners in the offer, e.g., the parents of Samson; 2) vows and public payment of the valuation by men called as prophets; 3) Levites who paid the valuation at the time they entered their service (Num. 4:23, 35, 43); and 4) women who ministered in a special way (Exod. 38:8). No substitutions were allowed, as in the case of the offer of property, and once the vow was made, that person was marked as turned over to the Lord. Worship in this sense was considered one of the highest privileges.

B. Dedication of Animals (vv. 9-13)

There were also those moments when people, in their worship, wanted to dedicate an animal from their flocks or herds, even an unclean one. Those presented as offerings, i.e., clean animals (v. 9), were regarded as holy and belonging to the Lord, and were never to be replaced or exchanged (v. 10). There were moments, however, when a person offered his best animal, and after reflecting upon it, had misgivings. Here the Lord taught the important lesson that one must pay what he had vowed to the Lord (Eccl. 5:4). There were also times when a person offered an inferior animal and then realized that he was a grudging giver, as the Spirit convicted him of stinginess. The Law was gracious and gave him opportunity to develop in giving-grace. The offerer could make a substitute, but then both the original offer and the substitute became holy to the Lord (v. 11). The Lord is indeed patient with us as we learn to give liberally to Him who so liberally gave to us.

Unclean animals, e.g., camels or donkeys, could also be brought to the priest, who then set a value on the animal, since it could not be offered on the altar (vv 11-12). But suppose the camel was choice, and the valuation set on it seemed too much to give. In these cases the offerer could arrange for a substitute animal, but this rearrangement took on the nature of a trespass (ch. 5), and one-fifth of the original valuation was added as a fine (v. 13). This became an object lesson: either follow through with the original intention, or pay for the lack of faith. The Lord has no respect for the latter attitude.

C. Dedication of Houses (vv. 14–15)

Provision was also made for the dedication of a house, whether it was a good one or a bad one. The priest evaluated it, and once the valuation was made, there could be no substitutions in case the offerer had second thoughts. However, if the person who offered the house wanted to redeem it, he had to pay the sanctuary the original evaluated price plus one-fifth extra.

D. Dedication of Fields (vv. 16–21)

There were times when a person wanted to dedicate a part of his fields to the Lord, and the valuation set by law was based on how much seed was needed to sow the fields, fifty shekels of silver for each homer (ten ephahs, or about six bushels) of barley seed, and any amount more or less proportionately evaluated (v. 16). An offerer would know beforehand what valuation he was giving to the Lord. If the offer was made right after the Year of Jubilee out of a grateful large-heartedness, the valuation stood at the appointed value until the next Jubilee, but if the offer was made some period of time after a Jubilee, a proportionately less valuation amount was fixed (v. 18). If the land was not redeemed by the original owner (by paying the one-fifth extra), or if he sold the land to another man (v. 20), the original owner could no longer redeem the field; rather, in the next Year of Jubilee, the land reverted to the priest because it was holy to the Lord. If land was devoted to the Lord by an Israelite, it could never be considered a loss because God will never be a debtor to any man! Land that was redeemed by an original owner, however, was never seen in a positive light by God, and the owner had to pay the consequences. Israel was encouraged to do her best for the Lord, and anything less than the best always betrayed a lack of faith and trust.

Owners who wished to dedicate land that did not belong to them by inheritance (v. 22) dedicated only the value of the land to the Year of Jubilee, and the offerer then presented this to the Lord. In this case the lesson taught was that he could give only what belonged to him and of that which was of value.

E. Standard of Value (v. 25)

It was now necessary to establish the standard of the shekel used to denote value. The phrase "the shekel of the sanctuary" was significant. No one could establish his own standard whereby the purchaser might make the value low and the seller would make it high. Some means of a standard measure of the shekel that would reflect God's holiness was entrusted to the priests. Right relations with the Lord demanded moral behavior in the handling of money for valuation.

F. That Which Belongs to the Lord (vv. 26–34)

Heretofore we have discussed voluntary vows, but there were properties that belonged to God, and they were to be offered at the appropriate time.

The first-born of animals could not be vowed since they already belonged to the Lord (Num. 18:15–18). The sons of Israel were to offer the first-born of clean animals to God as a thanksgiving offering, and all the remaining flesh of clean animals was to be food for the priests.

The first-born of unclean animals were in a different category. They too belonged to the Lord, and if they were not redeemed by the offerer, the priest set a valuation on them as if they had been offered to the Lord. The animals were then sold, and the money was the priest's. However, if the offerer redeemed it, he then paid the valuation set upon it and added the one-fifth extra; if he wanted it back, he had to pay dearly for it.

Property put under the ban (vv. 28–29)

In many instances property was "devoted," or put under the "ban," a particular English translation for a peculiarly used Hebrew word. The ban was considered more than a special vow, and property, people, and animals so marked were set for destruction, e.g., that which Achan took (Josh. 7:11, 20) and the Lord's ban on Agag and all that he and his followers represented (1 Sam. 15:3). However, gold, silver, bronze, and articles of iron might be put under the ban during times of attack against an enemy, in which case these articles were put into the treasury of the Lord (Josh. 6:19, 24). No soldier or officer was to appropriate any precious metal for himself when all such captured materials belonged to the Lord. The divine leadership was recognized, and no member of the armed forces was to gain personally from that which belonged to the Lord. In every case it was the Lord who called for the ban because there were times when He wanted to exhibit His holy judgment; in such cases His wrath fell on men who went beyond the point of no return in disobedience. We can only trust His wisdom in these matters.

The tithes of lands, trees, and beasts (vv. 30–33)

The Bible does not tell us the origin of the tithe. But Abraham gave the tithe to Melchizedek, and Jacob vowed the tithe at Bethel. Perhaps the tithe might be seen as the natural offering that belongs to the Lord out of the plenty He bestows on us. It appears, according to rabbinical suggestion that Israel under the Law had three tithes: 1) here in this passage is described the general tithe, the tithe that was paid to the Levites (Num. 18:21), 2) the tithe that was to be used in a sacred meal with offerer and Levite sharing (Deut. 14:22–27), and 3) the tithe every three years paid to the poor (Deut. 14:28–29). Some may be prone to be lax today in giving what belongs to the Lord, and we ought to ask, "If the sons of Israel gave three tithes under the Law, what should be our response in this age?"

In the general tithe the people were to tithe the produce of the land and the fruit of all the fruit trees. This is one tithe that could be redeemed since there might be instances when there was need for seed to sow fields again or to replenish fruit orchards. However, if there was a redemption, the value of the tithe plus one-fifth had to be paid, again indicating, in some way, the restoration of what belonged to the Lord.

In the tithe of flocks and herds, the tenth animal, whether it was a good or a bad one, was to be given to the Lord. No redemption was allowed here; every tenth belonged to the Lord without fail. If the animal was choice, the owner was to present it to the Lord with joy in His heart. However, if the animal was not choice, the owner could substitute for it another animal, although both animals then belonged to the Lord. In this regard God teaches us to be hilarious givers.

Conclusion (v. 34)

Leviticus ends with the emphasis that the foregoing commandments were those that the Lord had given to Moses on Sinai for the benefit of Israel. We can find benefit and blessing in them today. As we have said, too many Christians do not take time to delve into the great truths contained in this book that teaches the inner secrets of worship. If we would explore the deepest truths of the ministry and work of Jesus the Messiah, we must see the Book of Leviticus as a challenge to enrich Bible study. The precious truths of Jesus' life and atonement were already being enacted in the worship presented in that book. Leviticus clearly teaches us what John declared years later: because the Law was given through Moses, grace and truth can be realized through

Jesus Christ (John 1:17). We will rejoice through all eternity in the lessons of Leviticus that Jesus the Messiah fulfilled.

For Further Study

1. In a Bible dictionary or encyclopedia (see bibliography) read articles on: ban (dedication), shekel (weights, measures, and coins), tithe, vow.

2. Why were vows made in public?

3. Do we learn easily the grace of giving? Do you suppose God nudges believers today when they lose financially the very monies withheld from God?

4. Does the New Testament specify how much the believer should give today? Why?

5. How can we help believers to learn to give hilariously?

Bibliography

Commentaries on Leviticus

Allis, O. T., "Leviticus," *New Bible Commentary.* Davidson, F., ed. (Grand Rapids: Eerdmans, 1953).

Bonar, Andrew A. *A Commentary on the Book of Leviticus.* 5th ed. (London: Nisbet, 1875. Zondervan, 1959 reprint).

Bush, George. *Notes, Critical and Practical on Leviticus* (New York: Newman and Ivison, 1852. Klock, 1976 reprint).

Chapman, A. T. and Streave, A. W. *The Book of Leviticus* (Cambridge: University Press, 1914).

Erdman, Charles R. *The Book of Leviticus* (Westwood, N.J.: Revell, 1951).

Harrison, R. K. *Introduction to the Old Testament* (Grand Rapids: Eerdmans, 1969).

Jukes, A. *Law of Offerings in Leviticus, I-VII* (London: Nisbet, 1870).

Keil, C. F. and Delitzsch, F. *The Pentateuch in Biblical Commentary on the Old Testament,* Vol. II (Grand Rapids: Eerdmans, 1951 reprint).

Kellogg, S. H., "Leviticus," *Expositor's Bible,* Vol. I, 3rd ed. (London: Hodder and Stoughton, 1899. Eerdmans, 1947 reprint).

Kelly, W. *Day of Atonement* (London: Race, 1925).

_____. *Lectures on the Introduction to the Study of Leviticus* (London: Broom, 1871).

_____. *The Offerings of Leviticus,* I-VII (London: Weston, 1899).

Moller, Wilhelm, "Leviticus," *International Standard Bible Encyclopedia,* Vol. III. Eerdmans, 1952 reprint.

Murphy, James. *Commentary on Leviticus* (Andover: Draper, 1874).

Noth, M. *Leviticus, A Commentary*. Translated by J. E. Anderson (Philadelphia: Westminster, 1965).

Pentateuch and Hoftorahs, 2nd edition. Edited by J. H. Hertz (London: Soncino, 1971).

Pfeiffer, Charles. *The Book of Leviticus, A Study Manual* (Grand Rapids: Baker, 1957).

Ramban (Nachmanides). *Commentary on Leviticus*. Translated by Charles Chavel (New York: Shilo, 1979).

Seiss, Joseph. *Gospel in Leviticus (Philadelphia:Lindsay and Blakiston, 1860. Zondervan, n.d. reprint)*.

Wood, L. *A Survey of Israel's History* (Grand Rapids: Zondervan, 1970).

Young, E. J. *Introduction to the Old Testament*, revised (Grand Rapids: Eerdmans, 1965).

Bible Dictionaries and Encyclopedias

Buttrick, G. A., ed. *The Interpreter's Dictionary of the Bible*, 4 vols. (New York/Nashville: Abingdon Press, 1962).

Douglas, J. D., ed. *The New Bible Dictionary* (Grand Rapids: Eerdmans, 1970).

Orr, James, ed. *The International Standard Bible Encyclopedia*, 5 vols. (Grand Rapids: Eerdmans, 1957 reprint).

Tenney, Merrill C., ed. *The Zondervan Pictorial Bible Dictionary* (Grand Rapids: Zondervan, 1963).

_____ . *The Zondervan Pictorial Encyclopedia of the Bible*, 5 vols. (Grand Rapids: Zondervan, 1975).

Pfeiffer, Charles, Vos, Howard, and Rea, John, eds. *Wycliffe Bible Encyclopedia*, 2 vols. (Chicago: Moody Press, 1975).